M000207838

MEDITERRANEAN MOOD FOOD

MEDITERRANEAN
MOOD FOOD

What to eat to help beat depression and
live a longer, healthier life

PAULA MEE

GILL BOOKS

Gill Books
Hume Avenue
Park West
Dublin 12
www.gillbooks.ie

Gill Books is an imprint of M.H. Gill and Co.

© Paula Mee 2019

978 07171 8337 1

Designed by www.grahamthew.com
Photography © Joanne Murphy (www.joanne-murphy.com),
apart from pp. 5, 10, 15, 18, 22, 28, 34, 38, 41, 44, 47, 48, 65,
201 which are © Getty Images
Styled by Orla Neligan of Cornershop Productions (www.
cornershopproductions.com), assisted by Deborah Ryan
Cooking by Paula Mee and Clare Wilkinson
Copy-edited by Kristin Jensen
Proofread by Emma Dunne
Indexed by Eileen O'Neill
Printed by L&C Printing, Poland

PROPS
Meadows & Byrne: (01) 2804554/(021) 4344100;
www.meadowsandbyrne.com

Harvey Norman: (01) 4916300; harveynorman.ie

Marks & Spencer: (01) 2991300; www.marksandspencer.ie

Dunnes Stores: 1890 253185; www.dunnesstores.com

TK Maxx: (01) 2074798; www.tkmaxx.ie

Kathryn Davey Fabrics: kathryndavey.com

This book is typeset in Demo Next Pro Light, 9.5 on 14.5pt.

The paper used in this book comes from the wood pulp of
managed forests. For every tree felled, at least one tree is
planted, thereby renewing natural resources.

All rights reserved.

No part of this publication may be copied, reproduced or
transmitted in any form or by any means, without written
permission of the publishers.

A CIP catalogue record for this book is available
from the British Library.

5 4 3 2 1

Note to reader

This book is intended as a reference guide only, not as a medical manual. It is not a substitute for any medical or psychological treatment that may have been prescribed by your doctor. Bear in mind that nutritional needs vary from person to person. The information here is best used in conjunction with your dietitian or doctor.

About the author

PAULA MEE, BSc, Dip Dietetics, MSc in Health Sciences, MINDI, is a state-registered dietitian who lectures on a unique master's degree programme, the MSc in Applied Culinary Nutrition, in Technological University Dublin. Paula provides a range of health and wellness services to the food industry and corporate world. She contributes regularly to national media and is the co-author of *Gut Feeling* (2017) and *Your Middle Years: Love Them, Live Them, Own Them* (2016).

Acknowledgements

Thank you to my darling son Cian. Keep shining!

Thank you to JD for the wonderful MM breathers while writing.

Thanks also to Fiona Burke, whose executive coaching was so valuable.

And to my wonderful parents, siblings and friends – you are as always supportive and encouraging. I am very grateful to you all.

Thank you especially to Sarah Liddy for your gentle direction and reassurance. I am indebted to you and the Gill Books team, including Catherine Gough, Teresa Daly, Avril Cannon and colleagues. Thanks also to Kristin Jensen, Orla Neligan and Joanne Murphy. It was my great pleasure to work with you.

Every book is a collaborative undertaking. Without all the personal and professional support, *Mediterranean Mood Food* would never have made it!

Foreword

Mediterranean Mood Food is a decidedly timely publication. The role of diet and mood has until recent times been largely ignored by psychiatrists and other mental health professionals. However, in recent years the role of the brain-gut-microbiota axis has become an important topic for researchers and has provided the scientific basis for nutritional interventions, especially in mood-related disorders such as depression.

There is over one kilogram of bacteria in the adult human intestine, which in essence is equivalent to the weight of the human brain. Within this microbiota are a very diverse range of microbes, and published studies indicate that patients suffering from depression have less diversity of these microbes than normal healthy people. While the microbes undoubtedly produce molecules that our brain and other organs require, we provide the nutrients to enable them to flourish. In order to maintain a diverse microbiota, we need to take in a diverse range of foods. The Mediterranean diet is probably the optimal diet for maintaining gut health and subsequently mental health. It is also the diet most closely linked with longevity; there are more centenarians in Spain and Italy than anywhere else in Europe or North America. While genes play an important role in such longevity, so too does diet.

The diverse range of fruit and vegetables together with fish in the Mediterranean diet promotes microbial richness in the microbiota. Increasing evidence indicates that not only are those who consume a Mediterranean diet less likely to suffer from depression than those on a Northern European diet, but where depression does occur, antidepressant treatment is also likely to be more effective. Nutrition is seen as an adjunct to treatment and not an alternative to medication or psychological therapies.

How is a Mediterranean diet so effective in protecting mood? The answer to this question is at the heart of the current text. Depression is a disorder characterised by inflammation, and diet can be used to decrease this inflammatory process. The Mediterranean diet is rich in prebiotics, which promote the growth of good bacteria; polyphenols, which are antioxidant; and polyunsaturated fatty acids, which are a vital structural component in the brain as well as being anti-inflammatory.

This book is a highly practical introduction to the Mediterranean diet for maintaining good mental health. It is very clearly written and will undoubtedly be of benefit to a wide readership. Paula Mee is to be commended for her capacity to make relatively complex topics simple and for communicating her message in a clear and precise manner. For anyone interested in the topic of nutrition and mood, especially anyone prone to depression, this book is a must read.

TED DINAN
Professor of Psychiatry
University College Cork

Contents

Introduction: improve your mood with food

What if you could help your mental health, boost your mood and lower your risk of developing cognitive disorders in later life just by tweaking the way you eat?

For a life well lived, we need the right ingredients: fresh food, an active body and presence of mind. Of course, food isn't any more important than other health pillars. They all need to be intentionally integrated.

I'm a bit averse to the word 'diet', as it might suggest a short-term approach. This book has nothing to do with quick fixes or six-week solutions to our dietary troubles. Rather, it pinpoints the beneficial traits of more traditional ways of eating to present a plan for the long term: the Mediterranean Mood Food Plan (MMFP).

I want this book to be a guide to a sustainable long-term approach to health – an antidote to the growing number of fad diets out there and a straightforward, upfront approach to the cornerstones of good nutrition. This book is designed as a map for your journey towards improved mood and physical wellbeing, one meal at a time.

The MMFP is flexible and easy to follow and there's no need to count calories. Rather than a pyramid or plate, an MMFP is a flexitarian approach to enjoying healthy fats, fibre-rich carbohydrates and more plant proteins. That doesn't mean you can't enjoy a good steak or a delicious roast occasionally. However, the MMFP shapes your week to facilitate more frequent enjoyment of fibre-rich legumes or a fillet of smoked mackerel or salmon steak high in omega-3s.

A flexible meal pattern also allows for your own creativity to shine through. Fundamentally, you simply follow the 10 pillars (see pages 23-40) and build up a collection of recipes as you go in order to keep your plan as fresh and interesting as possible. There will be readers who are great chefs and cooks, so don't be shy about sharing your meal ideas on social media, but stick to the 10 pillars as carefully as you can.

As a dietitian, I have seen the benefits of this way of eating first-hand. I have witnessed the positive results and I understand the science behind them. I realise it can be a struggle to make good food choices and adapt your way of eating, but even simple improvements count. People who adhere to the MMFP can see significant decreases in blood glucose, blood pressure and cholesterol levels. These improvements all reduce the risk of heart disease and stroke. In addition, many patients report that they feel less hungry and are in better form following this pattern of eating – a far cry from the restrictive fad diets they have tried in the past. I have no way of telling if they experience improvement in cognitive function, but patients seem to be more confident in following this regime and simply sticking to it builds their confidence in making further positive lifestyle changes.

For many years we have known that the traditional Mediterranean diet (TMD) has numerous physical health benefits. However, the latest research reveals benefits for our mental health too. The brain accounts for just 2% of our body weight, but it uses up to 20% of our total daily calories. Although no single nutrient or food can boost brain health on its own, growing research shows that adherence to the TMD is associated with better brain health over time.

Both mental wellbeing and physical wellbeing shape our whole health. Mental health can't be sidelined. In fact, it must be prioritised.

There are many interactions between food, mood and mental health:

- What we eat can cause fluctuations in blood glucose levels, which in turn changes our mood and energy levels.
- Low intakes of essential fatty acids, vitamins and minerals can also affect our mental health.
- Particular deficiencies, such as certain B vitamin deficiencies, are linked to schizophrenia, while low levels of omega-3 fats are linked to depression.
- Neurotransmitters (serotonin, dopamine, acetylcholine and norepinephrine) are also dependent on what we eat and can influence how we think, feel and behave. These neurotransmitters help to regulate our mood, motivation, sleep, appetite, attention, arousal and feelings of pleasure. Some medications for depression target these brain chemicals.

Different foods in the diet have different effects on the microbiome (gut microbes) and the inflammatory response within the body. Highly refined, processed foods are pro-inflammatory, whereas other foods have an anti-inflammatory role. Over time, a pro-inflammatory diet can lead to a low-grade systemic inflammation affecting the whole body. There are marked increases in specific inflammatory cytokines or interleukins. These molecules cross the blood–brain barrier and interfere with numerous brain functions. For example, they can disrupt the availability of the neurotransmitter serotonin, which helps to regulate our mood and sleeping patterns. Inflammatory interleukins can also cause neurotoxicity and cell death in the brain by increasing the level of another neurotransmitter, glutamate.

So in other words, our pattern of eating can cause chronic low-grade inflammation in the body, and inflammation can in turn affect our brain function. In the long term, inflammation in the brain may increase the risk of cognitive impairment, Parkinson's disease, dementia and depression.

Media stories that blame individual foods such as white flour, sugar and sweeteners are a little misleading. Individually foods have little effect, but the pattern of food consumption over time really matters.

Carbohydrates, for example, receive a lot of negative press. Readers might be confused and unsure as to whether they should include or avoid them, so the first thing you need to understand is that the term 'carbohydrate' is an umbrella term.

- Digestible carbohydrates include starches and sugars. These are the preferred energy source for the brain and the working muscle. However, excess added sugar or free sugars are targeted for reduction.
- Indigestible carbohydrates (oligosaccharides, fibre and resistant starch) provide us with little energy, but they have many important functions. They help to move food and waste along the intestine; they slow down the digestion and absorption of glucose; and they are fermented by bacteria in the large intestine, which can help to regulate inflammation and the immune system.

Observational and intervention studies show that highly refined, Western-style diets (that are typically low in fibre) reduce the diversity of the microbiome. This results in a decrease in the number of protective bacteria that specialise in the fermentation of fibre and increases our gut exposure to pro-inflammatory chemicals that are produced by the not-so-good gut bacteria. This disruption in the microbiome balance can increase the risk of cancer.

What's flourishing in our colon has far-reaching effects

The microbiome–gut–brain axis is a fascinating emerging concept. Patterns of eating over time affect our microbiome and gut integrity and can ultimately impact our brain function.

The flexibility or malleability of our gut microbiome makes it possible to adopt a pattern of eating that might correct a microbial imbalance (dysbiosis) and restore health. According to *Molecular Psychiatry* (2018), 'There is a robust association between both higher adherence to a Mediterranean diet and lower adherence to a pro-inflammatory diet and a lower risk of depression.'

A recent meta-analysis of 21 studies, from 10 different countries, up to September 2016 confirmed the links between a more plant- and fish-based diet (high intakes of vegetables, fish, olive oil, whole grains, fruit and low-fat dairy) and a reduced risk of depression. The problem is our existing Western-style diet, which is high in processed and red meat, refined grains and sugar and high-fat dairy with little fruit and veg – it's not supporting our mental health.

Of course, like all disease, depression is linked to many different genetic and environmental factors. It's a complex interaction between brain chemicals, stress, genes, physical illnesses, poor lifestyle habits, certain drugs and hormones, but what we eat is one of the few factors that we can control and it seems it might be well worth the investment.

Key nutrients for the brain include omega-3 fatty acids and vitamin B12. There is good evidence that vitamin B12, found in seafood and dairy foods, is important for cognitive development. In observational studies, low levels of vitamin B12 are associated with cognitive decline and dementia in both adult and elderly groups. Vegetarians, especially vegans, are at risk of vitamin B12 deficiency, as only certain nutritional yeast products and fortified breakfast cereals contain vitamin B12. The TMD contains many natural sources of B12, such as fish, shellfish, poultry, eggs, dairy and the occasional meat dish.

Our brains are constantly making new brain cells and junctions between them, called synapses. Omega-3 fatty acids help to strengthen these connections by reducing inflammation, which weakens cognitive function.

Omega-3 fatty acids have been studied in a wide range of mood disorders with some interesting results. For example, an observational study in 2013 published in the *British Journal of Nutrition* found that subjects who consumed the most DHA (a type of omega-3 fatty acid found in oily fish) had up to a 50% reduced risk of anxiety disorders. We need more research about how they work, how effective they really are and their long-term safety for people managing mood and mental health conditions. Only then can conclusive recommendations be made about omega-3 supplementation.

In the meantime, focusing on naturally occurring omega-3 fatty acids in oily fish (salmon, mackerel, tuna, herring, sardines, anchovies, eel) is the best strategy. Eat oily fish at least once a week, preferably twice.

There is another key association between the TMD and the prevention of neurodegenerative diseases, including Alzheimer's disease and Parkinson's disease: it appears that the TMD can protect the brain from ageing and reduce the risk of degenerative diseases by approximately 10%. Although the research on the TMD and age-related cognitive decline is in its early stages, there is enough evidence to suggest that adhering to its principles is a good strategy to reduce cognitive decline and our risk of dementia.

The traditional Mediterranean diet (TMD) and disease

The TMD is not just good for our mental health. In the Seven Countries Study, one of the first large studies to explore the links between diet and disease, scientists looked at the health outcomes of nearly 13,000 middle-aged men in the United States, Japan, Italy, Greece, the Netherlands, Finland and then-Yugoslavia. They discovered that men from Crete in particular experienced lower cardiovascular disease rates than their counterparts in other countries. This was attributed to the men's simple post-war food choices, which emphasised fruits, vegetables, grains, beans and fish. This was the original TMD, although in recent years the definition has broadened in the scientific literature.

In an addendum to the Seven Countries Study, the research team described the 'low-coronary-risk male' living on the Isle of Crete as follows:

He is a shepherd or small farmer, a beekeeper or fisherman, or a tender of olives or vines. He walks to work daily and labors in the soft light of his Greek isle, midst the droning of crickets and the bray of distant donkeys, in the peace of his land. ... His midday, main meal is of eggplant, with large livery mushrooms, crisp vegetables, and country bread dipped in the nectar that is golden Cretan olive oil. Once a week there is a bit of lamb, naturally spiced from grazing in thyme-filled pastures. Once a week there is chicken. Twice a week there is fish fresh from the sea. Other meals are hot dishes of legumes seasoned with meats and condiments. The main dish is followed by a tangy salad, then by dates, Turkish sweets, nuts, or succulent fresh fruits. A sharp local wine completes this varied and savory cuisine. This living pattern, repeated six days a week, is climaxed by a happy Saturday evening. The ritual family dinner is followed by relaxing fellowship with peers. Festivity builds to a passionate midnight dance under the brilliant moon in the field circle where the grain of the region is winnowed. ... He is handsome, rugged, kindly—and virile. His is the lowest heart-attack risk, the lowest death rate, and the greatest life expectancy in the Western world.

Compared to other Western diets, the TMD was considered somewhat of an enigma. Although fat levels were higher (accounting for 40% of calories), the prevalence of heart disease, stroke, obesity and cancer was lower. Rather than limiting total fat intake, the TMD focused primarily on fat quality – the TMD was largely made up of unsaturated fats. At its core were monounsaturated fats found in olive oil, nuts and avocados. Also on the menu were polyunsaturated fats, found in oily fish.

It is both significant and interesting that fish dishes outnumbered meat or chicken dishes. The little lamb they had was organically flavoured by the thyme, herbs and grasses that the animals grazed on. Small portions of meat might occasionally be used to top up a legume dish, not the other way around. Vegetables, lentils and beans were their staples.

Desserts were naturally sweetened by adding ripened seasonal fruits or dried fruits like dates and figs. The quince, pistachio and nutty mixtures of many desserts were also sweetened with wild local honey, not refined sugar. Even though both honey and sugar break down into glucose molecules, local honey possesses antimicrobial properties that refined table sugar doesn't have.

What health benefits are associated with the TMD?

Association is not causation, but there are many well-conducted studies connecting the TMD to a range of health benefits. Again, there isn't one singular food or nutrient that stands out as better than others. Think about this as a pattern of eating or a synergistic combination of nutrients in a variety of foods. It's not about singular super nutrients, even though some are mentioned below.

A remarkable amount of solid research points to an impressive and expansive range of health benefits associated with the TMD, such as:

- Increased levels of antioxidants and decreased inflammation
- Reduced risk of type 2 diabetes
- Better blood sugar management in patients with existing type 2 diabetes
- Improved bone health
- Reduced risk of certain cancers
- Decreased risk of heart disease and stroke
- Slower cognitive decline with age
- Lower risk of depression and Alzheimer's disease in older age

Heart health

Some researchers suggest that the TMD can reduce the risk of heart attack and stroke within a matter of months. Certainly, in the aftermath of a heart attack the TMD has been shown to be almost three times more effective at reducing deaths as taking a statin (a common class of cholesterol-lowering medications). The pairing of an unsaturated fat (olive oil, avocado or nuts) with a green leafy salad produces anti-inflammatory nitro fatty acids, which help to protect blood vessels and promote a healthy blood flow.

Severity of psoriasis and other chronic inflammatory diseases

A small study in 2015 evaluated the link between adherence to the TMD and the severity of psoriasis. It found a strong relationship between a higher consumption of extra virgin olive oil and a lower psoriasis severity.

The extra virgin olive oil not only contains omega-3 fatty acids, but also several antioxidant polyphenols and vitamin E, which protect against chronic inflammatory disease. Polyphenols are a group of about 500 phytonutrients that are found naturally in plants. Flavonoids and phenolic acid are just two examples. Their health benefits are linked to their antioxidant function: they mop up free radicals that damage our cells and tissues. Scientists are researching their ability to influence our gut bacteria, genes and gene expression. Everyday herbs and vegetables such as onion, garlic, capers, parsley, dill and chives contain flavonoids and allicin. Crushing garlic cloves just 15 minutes before cooking can help to maximise the antioxidant benefits of the released allicin.

Cancer

In a meta-analysis published in the *British Medical Journal*, which collectively included more than 1.5 million participants, the researchers found that greater adherence to a TMD resulted in significant improvements to health, including a 9% drop in overall mortality; a 9% drop in mortality from cardiovascular disease; a 6% reduction in incidence of or mortality from neoplasm (the abnormal growth of tissue in a part of the body), which is a characteristic of cancer; and a 13% reduction in incidence of Parkinson's disease and Alzheimer's disease.

Weight management

Higher fibre intakes are associated with healthier weights too. Soluble fibres help us to feel full and reduce our appetite, which in turn can help us to lose weight.

In a recent study published in the *American Journal of Clinical Nutrition*, 21 healthy adults with an average fibre intake were given one fibre-rich snack bar (with 21g of fibre) each day for three weeks. The study found that the subjects significantly increased their levels of gut bacteroidetes and decreased their levels of gut firmicutes compared with levels before the study or after three weeks of eating fibre-free bars. This shift in the ratio of having more fibre-loving gut bacteroidetes to fewer firmicutes was associated with a lower body mass index (BMI).

Bone health

Good nutrition is critical to build and maintain optimal bone mass and to prevent osteoporosis. Previously, calcium and vitamin D were considered to be the main nutrients in the fight against bone disease. Now, it appears that vitamins A, B, C, E and K and minerals such as potassium, magnesium and silicon may all influence bone health.

Preliminary results of a study in 2017 suggest that strong adherence to the TMD promotes bone health as we age and that we can use this pattern of eating to help prevent inflammatory disease, such as osteoporosis. The anti-inflammatory properties of polyphenols found in extra virgin olive oil, vegetables, fruits, legumes and red wine are thought to be key in the TMD.

Ageing and telomere length

The TMD may stop the DNA code from scrambling as people age, according to a study published in the *British Medical Journal*. Boston researchers followed nearly 5,000 nurses for over a decade. Nurses who followed the TMD seemed to safeguard their telomeres, which are protective little caps at the ends of our chromosomes that prevent the loss of genetic information when the cell is dividing. When telomeres get shorter, the chromosomes' structure deteriorates and the DNA can get scrambled.

Shorter telomeres are associated with a wide range of age-related diseases, including our biggest killers: heart disease and cancers. Longer telomeres are associated with slower ageing.

What is the best way to eat for you personally?

There's no easy answer to this question, as people respond differently to the same food. Scientists who tracked 800 subjects over a week continuously monitored their blood sugar levels in response to foods and found that identical meals had a different impact on every person. A bowl of brown rice caused a worse spike in blood glucose levels than a bowl of ice cream in some individuals.

The impact of food on health can't be measured purely by assessing the nutrient value of what people eat. The impact is strongly influenced by how the nutrients we absorb along with other bioactive compounds influence our microbiome and how the substances produced by the microbiome may switch our genes on and off.

The emerging field of nutritional psychiatry is also working out how certain gut bacteria influence our food choices and how that makes us feel and behave. Prebiotics, probiotics and symbiotics (see below) will be key in beneficially manipulating and enhancing the microbiome in the coming years.

Probiotics and prebiotics

PROBIOTICS

Probiotics are live bacteria found naturally in some foods, food supplements and in the gut. They improve our health by competing with and reducing the number of harmful microbes in the gut. Probiotics help us to make B and K vitamins and the happy gut hormone, serotonin. They also produce anti-inflammatory short chain fatty acids (SCFAs) and substances that are linked to improved immune function. Some research suggests they may even protect against obesity. We can boost our gut levels of transitory healthy probiotics by eating live probiotic and fermented foods.

Fermented vegetables such as sauerkraut and pickles are popular supermarket items, but you can ferment your own vegetables at home. *The Cultured Club* by Dearbhla Reynolds can be a great addition to your recipe book repertoire.

When buying yogurt, look for words such as 'live' or 'active' on the labels to ensure that the manufacturing process hasn't killed the probiotic strains. Natural or Greek yogurts are good options for cooking or as a dessert topping.

PREBIOTICS

Prebiotics are fibres and resistant starches that are used as fuel by the good bacteria in the colon. We don't digest them ourselves – our gut bacteria ferment them. It's a win-win situation. Bacteria ferment the fibres we don't need and in turn provide us with many health and immune benefits. Foods that contain these probiotic fibres include:

- **Legumes:** All types of beans, chickpeas and lentil
- **Nuts:** All types of nuts and nut butters

- **Vegetables:** Many vegetables, especially endive, leek, asparagus, garlic, onion and artichokes
- **Fruit:** Apples, pears, peaches, plums, nectarines and dried fruit (e.g. dates, figs)
- **Whole grains:** Barley, rye, wheat, oats, farro

Symbiotics

We humans have a symbiotic relationship with the microbes in our guts. We don't possess the enzymes to break down fibre, so it escapes digestion in the small intestine and continues down into the large intestine (colon), where the fibre can be broken down by bacteria with a wider range of enzymes.

The fibre in some foods can be broken down by the bacteria relatively quickly. This type of fibre is called soluble or rapidly fermentable fibre and is digested in the upper part of the large intestine (colon). Other fibres are very difficult to break down and they travel much further down the large intestine before bacteria can act on them. These fibres are known as insoluble or poorly fermentable fibre.

At present we eat too many highly processed foods with little fibre. This essentially starves the good bacteria in the gut. Some die, while researchers hypothesise that others consume the protective mucus barrier separating our human cells from the microbiome. The interactions between microbes and human cells may cause immune dysregulation, inflammation and disease. Disruption of the microbiome is associated with many inflammatory and autoimmune conditions.

One outcome is certain: a poor fibre intake reduces the diversity and number of protective bacteria producing short chain fatty acids (SCFAs) in the gut. These SCFAs have multiple roles in:

- Reducing inflammation, boosting immunity and protecting against bowel cancer
- Improving nutrient absorption from the gut
- Regulating our mood
- Lowering anxiety levels and the risk of depression

A life-saving meal pattern

Individual nutrients and supplements aren't lifesavers, but meal patterns may be. The TMD gives us insights into meal patterns that are associated with good health and longevity.

Important benefits of the TMD come from its antioxidant and anti-inflammatory effects. Inflammation and oxidative stress (an imbalance between the production of free radicals and the body's ability to counteract their harmful effects) are at the root of all disease. High intakes of oily fish, whole grains and plant foods boost soluble fibre, minerals, vitamins and phytonutrients, which have protective effects.

If we take a reductionist approach and try to identify anti-inflammatory nutrients, it seems there are many plant phytochemicals (including carotenoids and anthocyanins) that have anti-inflammatory effects due to their antioxidant roles. Antioxidants mop up free radicals and protect tissues from damage and prevent unwanted inflammatory responses.

To that end, try to include as many of these foods in the Mediterranean Mood Food Plan (MMFP) as you can:

- Apples
- Red berries
- Blueberries
- Kiwis
- Cherries
- Citrus fruit
- Onions
- Aubergines
- Sweet potatoes
- Spinach
- Purslane
- Green tea
- Olives and olive oil
- Beans and legumes
- Oily fish
- Nuts

How to follow the Mediterranean Mood Food Plan

The following are the nutrition principles of the MMFP:

1 It is high in unsaturated fats (monounsaturated fat – olive oil, nuts, avocado – and polyunsaturated fat – oily fish, chia seeds, linseeds); low in saturated fats (animal fats and meat products, palm and coconut oils); and contains little or no trans fats (deep-fried foods, processed long-life foods).
2 It is high in unrefined, fibre-rich carbohydrates (vegetables, fruits, whole grains, herbs) and low in highly refined carbohydrates (confectionary, sweets, chocolate, biscuits, cakes, white bread, white rice, crisps).
3 It is high in plant proteins (legumes – such as peas, beans and lentils – nuts and seeds) and low in animal protein (meat and highly processed meat products). It includes regular moderate consumption of animal proteins such as cheese and natural or Greek yogurt.

Currently our Western diet contains excessive red and processed meats (salami, bacon, etc.), refined grains in white bread and sugary breakfast cereals, desserts, soft drinks and fried foods. This leads to higher levels of pro-inflammatory cytokines and lower levels of anti-inflammatory cytokines in the body.

Chronic inflammation is also linked to obesity. Fat tissue releases hormones and pro-inflammatory cytokines, adding to the risk of chronic diseases such as cardiovascular disease, type 2 diabetes, cancer, dementia and Alzheimer's disease. Conversely, a Mediterranean-style eating plan, rich in antioxidants, fibre and healthy fats, can reduce inflammation and provide numerous health benefits, including brain health.

Brain health

The MMFP is designed to support your brain health. The recipes are predominantly plant based, with the occasional meat dish included. If you adhere to the MMFP and its 10 pillars, you don't need to worry about counting calories or macronutrients (percentages of carbs, fats and proteins). You can be sure you are getting adequate vitamins, minerals and fibre to selectively feed the healthy bacteria in your microbiome. You don't have to be consciously concerned about the balance of your fats either. Fats are naturally and perfectly balanced in the components of a plant-rich diet (think avocados, nuts, seeds, olives and rapeseed and olive oils).

Unfortunately, there will be times when we honestly think we are complying and trying, but we clearly are not! Don't allow this to happen. You need to intentionally check in with yourself and consciously follow the 10 pillars – at least initially to break older, unhelpful habits. There isn't one right way to do this, so find one that works for you. For example, could a smartphone reminder before each meal help to ground you? Is there an app to help you shop, prepare and store MMFP-style recipes that you collect? Half-following the advice can provide some positive health outcomes, but if you are going to use the MMFP, start by embracing the concept fully and cement the new principles, then allow yourself the occasional diversion.

Frequently recall your short-term goals. This will help nudge you to make better food choices. If you are over 40 years old, ask your doctor to test your blood pressure and blood lipid profile at week 1 and week 12 as you follow the MMFP. Monitoring and measuring these hidden benefits can be very motivating.

Broader benefits

The EAT-Lancet Commission report 2019 confirms that food is the single strongest lever we have to improve human health and environmental sustainability on Earth. The commission, using quantitative scientific targets, shows that feeding 10 billion people on a healthy diet within safe planetary boundaries for food production by 2050 is both achievable and essential.

Substantial changes need to be made: we need to more than double the consumption of fruits, vegetables, legumes and nuts, and have a greater than 50 per cent reduction in global consumption of red meat and foods containing added sugar.

The 10 pillars of the Mediterranean Mood Food Plan

Here's how and why to adopt some of the traditional habits of Mediterranean countries.

1. Eat more vegetables and fruit

WHAT TO EAT: Aim to eat five vegetables and two fruits each day. Most people need to increase their consumption of vegetables and fruit. Include lots of colour on your plate. Make it a goal to eat a minimum of one green vegetable each day.

A popular TMD salad leaf was wild purslane. It tastes a bit like spinach or watercress and is one of the few leafy green vegetables that contains omega-3 fatty acids. It also contains vitamins, the antioxidant glutathione, minerals and pectin, a soluble fibre. Purslane is difficult to get these days, but you could grow your own in a garden pot. Pinch off a few leaves to toss into salads or sandwiches. Rocket is easy to grow too.

Skip the white toast. Toss a handful of spinach on top of your poached eggs for the last 30 seconds of their cooking time or into your olive oil-coated pan if you're frying an egg. Top your open sandwich or homemade pizza with a couple of handfuls of peppery rocket. Enjoy slices of green pepper with an aubergine or bean dip (pages 75 and 73). Blend a few handfuls of spinach into some Greek yogurt, then add chopped chives, a pinch of salt and the juice of half a lime to make a quick dip.

Certain greens are bitter and challenging to include. Add a handful of strawberries or blueberries for some natural sweetness in a watercress and rocket salad. Roast some grape halves with olive oil and herbs, then toss some kale into the grapes and heat the lot for 2 minutes.

In the TMD, wild greens and leaves were collected from a wide variety of plants, including thistle, dandelion, stinging nettle, mallow and purslane. These were eaten raw or boiled and served with lemon juice and olive oil. If foraging wild leaves and herbs isn't for you, include lots of cultivated commercial herbs and leaves as a garnish on sandwiches, in salads, when cooking and even in your water bottle. Better yet, grow your own in a little planter. Look online for suitable help and instructions.

WHY IS IT SO GOOD? Most vegetables and fruits are low in calories. They also have a low glycaemic load, so they don't make your blood sugar levels spike and crash. They also contain bioactive nutrients in addition to the essential vitamins and minerals that have antioxidant and anti-inflammatory properties.

Many vegetables and fruits are also prebiotics (see the definition on page 14). They contain non-digestible oligosaccharides (carbohydrates), which selectively help to fuel the good bacteria in the microbiome. These prebiotics are typically found in garlic, leeks, onions, spring onions, artichokes, asparagus and dark leafy green veggies.

PREBIOTIC SUPPLEMENTS: Eating veg, fruit and whole grains is probably the best way to keep your microbiome healthy. A growing number of prebiotic supplements are also appearing in pharmacies. A prebiotic supplement is defined as 'a substrate that is selectively utilised by host micro-organisms conferring a health benefit' – in other words, the supplement preferentially feeds or fuels protective gut bacteria. Health gains are evolving, but they currently include gut benefits (immune stimulation), heart benefits (blood lipid levels) and bone benefits (improved mineral bioavailability).

PROBIOTIC SUPPLEMENTS: These are strain specific, with some new formulations on the market. Zenflora is an interesting new supplement containing 1714-Serenitas, a unique culture that has been clinically studied in people with everyday stress. It offers support for the mind and body during busy and demanding times. It also contains biotin, folate, niacin, thiamine, B6 and B12, which contribute to normal psychological function.

FRUITS: Eat prebiotic whole fruits regularly, such as blueberries, pears, watermelons and nectarines. If you don't eat fruit between meals, include it as part of a lighter meal, for example farmhouse cheese with a sliced apple, a fresh fig or a handful of grapes.

Well-known phytonutrients include carotenoids (which make apricots orange) and anthocyanins (which make blueberries blue). In addition to pigments, phytonutrients also impart flavours and aromas. Fruit is a good source of vitamin C, which can help to prevent cell damage.

2. Eat more legumes, nuts and seeds

WHAT TO EAT: Eat an average serving (90g) of different legumes four times per week. Legumes are plants that grow in pods (such as French beans). Pulses are only the edible seeds inside the pods (such as beans, lentils and chickpeas), so pulses are part of the legume family.

We need to increase our intake of legumes. Replacing red meat with plant proteins brings economic, environmental and health benefits. Tinned pulses contain much the same nutritional benefits as dried varieties, plus they are inexpensive and convenient. Don't be afraid of them if you haven't tried them before. They are not strong tasting – in fact, many of them are quite bland and merge with the flavours you use in a dish, dressing or sauce. Enhance soups by adding butter beans or toss lentils into casseroles or salads. Instead of crisps, make a batch of roasted chickpeas for a delicious, filling snack during the week.

If you don't normally eat these foods, increase them slowly and eat small portions regularly. Allow some time for your digestive system to accept them. Excess wind will diminish in time as your microbiome adapts. If you have irritable bowel syndrome (IBS) and feel that pulses cause digestive discomfort and other symptoms, discuss the short intervention, low FODMAP diet with a qualified dietitian (for more information on the low FODMAP diet, see *Gut Feeling*, a book I co-authored with Kate O'Brien).

WHAT NUTS AND SEEDS SHOULD YOU EAT? Eat a handful of mixed nuts (25g) in meals or as a snack four times per week. Garnish, flavour and add texture to your dishes with plain unsalted or toasted nuts and seeds. Try to avoid commercial nut and seed mixes with added flavourings and sugar-coated caramelised versions.

WHY IS IT SO GOOD? Legumes, pulses, nuts and seeds are among the most versatile and nutritious plant proteins available. They contain protein and fibre as well as many essential minerals and vitamins. They have a low glycaemic index, which helps to keep your blood sugars stable. They are one of the best sources of soluble fibre, which has a prebiotic effect, selectively feeding good bacteria in the microbiome. Because they also contain many essential amino acids, a selection of legumes, pulses, nuts and seeds is a versatile alternative to red meat during the week.

Don't be concerned about the fat in nuts. Most of it is unsaturated (both monounsaturated and polyunsaturated), which can lower 'bad' cholesterol levels. Nuts and seeds also contain soluble fibre and plant sterols, which can help to lower cholesterol. Almonds are high in vitamin E, pumpkin seeds are high in L-arginine and walnuts are high in omega-3 fatty acids. These nutrients help to improve the flexibility of artery walls and stop the development of plaque, which restricts blood flow.

Brazil nuts are high in selenium, an important nutrient for a healthy thyroid. Of all the nuts, walnuts are the best source of an omega-3 fatty acid called alpha-linolenic acid (ALA). A 2015 UCLA study linked higher walnut intakes with improved cognitive test scores. This type of fatty acid can also help to lower blood pressure and protect arteries, so both the brain and heart benefit. But remember, if the nuts and seeds you eat are always sugar coated or smothered in chocolate or salt, this can negate their health benefits.

Quinoa is the edible seed of a flowering amaranth plant. It's an excellent plant protein, as it contains all nine essential amino acids (as do soya beans, although they're not a Mediterranean staple). Red quinoa is my favourite. It looks great, has a nutty texture and cooks faster than rice.

However, while some seeds and nuts contain ALAs, it isn't converted into the components we need for heart, brain and joint health as well as the omega-3 fatty acids found in fish.

3. Eat more olive oil

WHAT TO EAT: Use olive oil as your primary fat. Enjoy 1 to 2 tablespoons per day (maybe less if you are also trying to lose weight).

A better balance of fats can improve our health. Replace saturated fat and trans fats with some monounsaturated fat. Although traditionally Mediterranean people consumed relatively high amounts of fat, they had lower rates of cardiovascular disease than the rest of the Westernised world. Their total fat intake was typically up to 40% of their total calories, but saturated fat accounted for only 8%. This is in clear contrast to our modern-day pattern of eating, where we fail to find a healthy balance between unsaturated and saturated fat.

Use olive oil to enhance the flavour of a salad or in a marinade for seafood. Nibble on olives as a pre-dinner snack. Enjoy extra virgin olive oil with a few drops of balsamic vinegar added to it for dipping in some sourdough bread.

WHY IS IT SO GOOD? The beneficial effects of olive oil are essentially due to two components: omega-9 monounsaturated fatty acid (oleic acid) and antioxidant substances (for example, vitamin E and phenolic compounds). Positive benefits include:

· A reduction of total and low-density lipoprotein (LDL) cholesterol (L for lousy)
· A possible increase in high-density lipoprotein (HDL) cholesterol (H for healthy)
· A decrease in the oxidation of LDL cholesterol
· A reduction in inflammation
· A reduction in plaque formation
· Improvement in blood pressure
· Improvement in blood clotting mechanisms

The best grade is extra virgin olive oil, which is made from the first pressing of the olives. Once they have been hand picked, they are brought to mills where they are pressed that same day. The entire olive is used to make the oil: pulp, skin and even the husk. The olives are crushed by mechanical stainless steel grindstones to produce an olive paste.

The cold press method allows olive oil to maintain its flavour, colour and nutritional value. In fact, olive oil is the only oil that can be consumed as it is removed from the fruit, with no need for further processing. Because no other chemical processing is involved, the oil retains the natural vitamins, minerals, antioxidants and other healthy products of the olive fruit.

Extra virgin olive oil is much richer in antioxidants than lower-grade oils, but you could vary its use at home with macadamia nut oil or avocado oil.

4. Eat more oily fish

WHAT TO EAT: Eat at least one portion (or two if possible) of oily fish every week. Avoid larger, longer-living fish (shark, swordfish) with higher levels of tissue contaminants such as mercury and **polychlorinated biphenyls** (PCBs). Choose smaller, shorter-lived fish (anchovies, salmon, sardines) instead. You can also enjoy a fillet of white fish or some shellfish during the week, although they don't offer the benefits of the omega-3 fatty acid in oily fish.

We need to eat more fish, but especially oily fish. Access to fish today is good, although wild stock is unavailable unless it's a sustainable species. Farmed and frozen oily fish don't taste quite as good, but they still contain vital omega-3 fatty acids and vitamin D.

WHAT ABOUT TINNED TUNA? There are seven varieties of tuna you might buy: albacore, bigeye, skipjack, yellowfin, Atlantic bluefin (farmed and wild), southern bluefin (farmed and wild) and Pacific bluefin. However, it's best to avoid all bluefin varieties. The best tuna variety to choose is generally skipjack, a fast-growing species that is still quite plentiful around the world and accounts for most of the tinned tuna on supermarket shelves. Controlling the mercury content of tinned tuna comes down to controlling the size and age of the fish used. Skipjack tuna is lower in mercury.

Tinned tuna has lower mercury levels than tuna steaks and sushi. Two tinned tuna meals a week is a safe threshold according to the US Food and Drug Administration (FDA). The Food Safety Authority of Ireland (FSAI) recommends that pregnant women limit their tuna intake to one fresh tuna steak (≤150g) or 2 x 240g cans of tinned tuna per week due to its mercury content. Overall, the better option is tinned salmon. It is very low in mercury and much higher in beneficial omega-3s.

SUPPLEMENTS: Eicosapentaenoic acid (EPA) and docosahexaenoic acid (DHA) are omega-3 fatty acids found in oily fish that readily support our health. However, if you don't eat oily fish, pick up a vegetarian omega-3 fatty acid supplement that derives DHA from algae. These **supplements** are becoming more popular due to the growing interest in vegetarianism. Some combine the omega-3 fatty acids with vitamin D, which is an excellent idea if you don't eat oily fish, the only rich and natural source of these two nutrients.

WHY IS IT SO GOOD? Omega-3 fatty acids are polyunsaturated fatty acids and are required for building new brain cells and to strengthen the connections (synapses) between existing brain cells. These fats can also help to reduce inflammation, which impairs brain function.

Observational research suggests that people with the highest intake of DHA suffer less with anxiety disorders. Oily fish is a good source of DHA. The vegetarian sources of omega-3, such as chia seeds, linseeds and walnuts, contain alpha-linolenic acid (ALA), but only a small fraction of their fatty acids are converted to DHA.

Many of the health benefits of the TMD are thought to be related to a high intake of omega-3. The anti-inflammatory effects of omega-3 fatty acids help to reduce the risk of heart disease, cancer, dementia and Alzheimer's disease.

Oily fish is also an excellent source of vitamin D, which acts more like a hormone than a vitamin. It controls the concentration of calcium in the blood and is vital for strong bones, but it also influences brain function. A recent study in the *Journal of Psychiatry and Behavioral Sciences* found that the higher the vitamin D levels in young women, the lower their risk of anxiety.

Older people, too, need to ensure an adequate vitamin D intake. In the Irish Longitudinal Study of Ageing at Trinity College Dublin, vitamin D deficiency was associated with an increased risk of depression in over 75 per cent of older adults (December 2018).

The mineral iron helps to deliver oxygen to every cell in your body. It also helps to produce neurotransmitters and myelin sheaths, which protect nerve cells and allow them to signal to one another effectively. Inadequate intakes or increased needs due to heavy menstruation can cause iron deficiency anaemia, common symptoms of which include chronic tiredness, depression, brain fog and irritability.

The richest sources of iron in the TMD were seafood, poultry and the occasional meat dish, but these same sources together with egg yolks, nuts and beans can adequately boost levels in the MMFP.

5. Eat more herbs, spices and seaweed

WHAT TO EAT: Add home-grown herbs, organic seaweed, garlic, turmeric and other spices to your lunch and dinner daily. Reduce your intake of processed sauces and condiments, which have lots of added salt.

Sea vegetables, or seaweed, are rinsed thoroughly and dried at low temperatures to preserve their rich nutritional content. There are fabulous Irish companies such as Algaran, Wild Irish Sea Veg, Connemara Seaweed Company and smRt operating on the Wild Atlantic Way that have organic certification. This requires that all seaweed produced is free from contamination and regular analysis ensures that all seaweed products are safe and healthy to eat.

We are only beginning to find ways to include organic, sustainable sea vegetables in meals and snack foods. Here are some suggestions:

· Garnish your soup with strips of sea vegetables.
· Bake white fish with strips or sheets of sea vegetables (see the recipe for baked cod on a bed of ratatouille on page 150).
· Cook kombu strips with various beans for flavour and added minerals.
· Add sea spaghetti to a stir-fry.
· Use dulse/dillisk flakes as a salt substitute to sprinkle on breads or salad.
· Add spirulina or chlorella powder to a veggie smoothie.
· Blend dulse/dillisk or kelp into a salad dressing.
· Buy commercial snacks, such as Triantain, which bill themselves as Gaelic nachos with carrageen, or smRt bars made with dates, nuts, raisins and nori.
· Buy books such as *Irish Seaweed Kitchen* by Prannie Rhatigan or *Extreme Greens* by Sally McKenna for clever ways to include more sea vegetables.

WHY IS IT SO GOOD? Kelp, brown algae and other sea vegetables contain an anti-inflammatory component called fucoidan. Herbs and spices are also rich in antioxidants and have anti-inflammatory properties. Although we eat only minute quantities, if we include these ingredients daily, replacing salt and additive-laden processed ingredients, we can enhance the taste and health benefits of the MMFP.

Compared to surface-dwelling plants and vegetables, seaweeds are all-round good sources of fibre, omega-3 fatty acids, essential amino acids and vitamins A, B, C and E. Again, you only need to include a little, but often.

6. Eat moderate amounts of whole grains (more if you are active)

WHAT TO EAT: How much you eat will depend on how active you are. The basics of a complete meal include a good protein, some healthy fat and a wholegrain or high-fibre carbohydrate. Try some interesting carbohydrates, such as farro, barley, buckwheat, bulgur wheat, kamut, steel cut oats, quinoa (which is really a seed), brown rice, wild rice (which is really a grass) and sweet potatoes as well as staple cupboard items like 100% wholewheat flour.

If you buy bread, see if you can source a sourdough bread locally. Sourdough bread is made with a culture of wild, naturally occurring bacteria and yeast. The fermentation process produces a slightly sour-tasting bread and makes it easier to digest.

Enjoy 100% sourdough wholegrain bread instead of highly refined carbohydrates, such as white bread, processed breakfast cereals, white rice and chipped potatoes, which contain little or no fibre. This will help to increase your B vitamin intake as well as your fibre levels, which in turn helps to regulate blood sugar and insulin levels and also regulates your appetite more effectively.

Refined and highly processed carbohydrates can contain lots of simple sugars and calories, yet are nutrient poor. Eating too many refined carbohydrates can raise C-reactive protein (CRP) levels, which is a marker for inflammation.

Eat fewer whole grains and starchy carbs if you are overweight. Two to four servings with your seven fruits and vegetables each day will provide some good nutrition. Eat more (six plus) if you're more active and you need the energy.

ONE SERVING OF CARBOHYDRATE IS:
· One slice of bread (choose sourdough, wholegrain or seeded)
· Two wholegrain or high-fibre crackers
· Three dessertspoons of dry porridge oats or unsweetened muesli
· Three dessertspoons of quinoa or whole grains

WHY IS IT SO GOOD? Carbohydrates are an important source of energy for active people. They are also vital to produce serotonin (sometimes called the happy hormone). That's why following very low-carb or ketogenic diets can lower mood and energy levels.

However, the type of carbohydrate you eat is critical. Excessive intakes of refined carbohydrates and processed sugars are linked with inflammation, poor energy and mood swings. Choose wholegrain foods containing insoluble and soluble fibres.

Soluble fibre is a type of fibre that dissolves in water in the gut to form a gel-like substance. It not only keeps your gut healthy, but it can also help to lower levels of 'bad' cholesterol by soaking up the cholesterol like a sponge and carrying it out of the body.

Insoluble fibre is a type of fibre that does not dissolve in water. It helps with the movement of material through your digestive tract to prevent constipation. Good sources of insoluble fibre include high-fibre cereals and brans, wholegrain bread, and fruit and vegetables (including the skins).

Fibre, more than any other dietary component, has been empirically established as crucial for a healthy, diverse microbiome. Fibre is not found in any animal foods, even nutritious ones such as seafood, lean meats, poultry, eggs and dairy. It is only found in plant-based foods such as whole grains, legumes, pulses, fruit and vegetables.

Simply replacing refined grains (such as white bread or white rice) with whole grains (such as wholegrain bread or porridge) can have a significant impact on your health. A study published in the *American Journal of Clinical Nutrition* in 2017 randomly assigned 81 healthy adults to eat either whole grains or refined grains for six weeks, controlling all other foods and nutrients between the groups. The researchers found that the wholegrain diet led to a higher concentration of good gut bacteria and SCFAs, which is a gauge of good colon health. The wholegrain group also notably improved their metabolism over the six-week study compared with the refined grains group, burning 92 more calories per day without exercising more.

While the science of the gut microbiome is still in its infancy, the benefits of a fibre-rich pattern of eating are very favourable.

7. Eat moderate amounts of probiotic foods, such as live natural yogurt and other fermented foods

WHAT TO EAT: We can help shape our microbiome through our everyday diet. Include two to three servings of fermented dairy foods, which are rich in probiotics, every day. A serving is a small 125g carton of live natural or Greek yogurt. Good bacteria can survive in cheeses such as cottage cheese and mozzarella as well as in some aged cheeses, such as Parmesan. An average serving is 25g of cheese. Kefir is a fermented milk that you can make at home or buy commercially. A serving is 200ml.

Prebiotics (from your veggies and whole grains) and probiotics (from fermented foods) work together synergistically. For example, prebiotics are the foods that fuel the gut's probiotics, which ultimately can improve or restore gut microbe balance. Good combos include blueberries and live yogurt or roasted asparagus with Parmesan shavings.

WHY IS IT SO GOOD? Probiotic **supplements** may also help to alleviate symptoms of depression in some people. Connections between the gut and brain (the gut–brain axis) are the focus of ongoing research, but it looks like gut health can affect our sleep patterns, anxiety levels and risk of depression. Although probiotic supplements show some promise, the evidence base is weak and future studies are necessary to identify which types of probiotics are most effective. However, eating probiotic foods containing live cultures of good bacteria is a good dietary habit as we wait for emerging science to guide us.

Years ago we consumed a lot of buttermilk, but today we can enjoy active cultures daily in various dairy foods that offer other bone minerals too. Dairy contains a matrix of minerals, vitamins and proteins that contribute to bone health. If you can't or don't want to eat moderate amounts of cow's, sheep's or goat's cheese, milk and yogurt, then make sure you choose from a range of fortified plant-based alternatives instead.

8. Eat up to seven eggs per week

WHAT TO EAT: Eat up to seven eggs per week. Include chicken, duck or quail eggs if they are available. Traditional Mediterranean people lived without refrigeration, but chickens and ducks were the gift that kept giving. They produced a consistent, steady stream of fresh eggs with high-quality protein, an excellent replacement for red meat.

WHY IS IT SO GOOD? Eggs contain a good selection of nutrients that are needed for the regular functioning of brain cells and the nervous system. Egg yolks contain choline, which is converted to acetylcholine, a neurotransmitter that helps to support memory and allows brain

cells to communicate effectively with each other. Eggs also contain B vitamins, such as thiamine, riboflavin, folate, B6, B12 and biotin. These vitamins not only help us to release energy from our food, but they are also closely linked to mood and cognitive function throughout life.

9. Eat less red meat and processed meat

WHAT TO EAT: Eat red meat only once a week and try to eat meat from grass-fed animals. Enjoy small portions (150g) and stretch out the meat with added pulses or legumes. People following the TMD ate meat only occasionally – approximately three times a month.

WHY IS IT SO GOOD? In the TMD, animals were grass fed and the red meat that people enjoyed was lean. The red meat produced in this way was also higher in anti-inflammatory omega-3 fatty acids. Chickens were free to roam and peck at seeds and insects, which in turn increased the omega-3 fatty acids in chicken meat and eggs.

When red meat is digested, it is broken into its component amino acids. These amino acids are involved in building proteins and neurotransmitters that allow brain cells to communicate effectively with one another. Dopamine is produced from the amino acid tyrosine and serotonin is produced from the amino acid tryptophan. Inadequate levels of these neurotransmitters impact our mental health.

We can get all nine essential amino acids in red meat, but we can also get them in fish, dairy and eggs. Quinoa is a good plant source containing all nine essential amino acids. Red meat is also a good source of iron and zinc. The advice is that a little red meat goes a long way and that we should keep processed meats to an absolute minimum.

10. Eat less processed, refined carbs and sugars

WHAT TO EAT: Minimise your intake of cakes, biscuits, pastry and confectionery as much as possible. If you drink alcohol, a maximum of one to two alcoholic drinks per day is recommended. Enjoy a glass of wine or two with your evening meal.

WHY IS IT SO GOOD? The combination of ethanol and phenolic compounds in red wine is thought to be good for the heart and circulatory system. Moreover, the synergistic effects of wine and olive oil together are even better (red wine seems to be higher in antioxidants and phenolic compounds than white).

Red wine contains resveratrol, an antioxidant found in the skin of red grapes. While Greeks drank moderate amounts of red wine, there is no need to take up drinking if you don't already do so. There are other ways to increase your resveratrol intake – foods high in this antioxidant include peanuts (choose unsalted) and purple grapes.

What most of us will need to limit

Personally, I don't think anyone should have to count calories. I think a better approach is to make more conscious food choices, skip certain less nutritious foods that are linked to weight gain and not overindulge. Having said that, though, most of us will still need to limit the following foods and drinks.

- **Sugary foods and drinks:** This involves reducing your consumption of white sliced pan, white rice, white pasta, sweet foods (desserts and treats) and sugary drinks (including soft drinks, energy and sports drinks, and freshly squeezed or commercial fruit juices). Instead, you can use ripened whole fruits (with skins where possible) to sweeten desserts and snacks. If you really like fruit juice, drink no more than 125ml a day. Better yet, just use fruit juices to add flavour or naturally sweeten the occasional dessert.
- **Potato portions (baked or fried):** Boil baby potatoes (with skins) instead of baked or fried versions and enjoy occasionally. Use a diverse range of whole grains or high-fibre carbohydrates, such as wholegrain barley in soups and casseroles, millet, amaranth, wheat berries, quinoa, wild rice and steel cut or full-flake oats. Bulk up your plate with extra veg, always putting green veg centre stage.
- **Red meats (beef, pork, lamb) and processed meats (bacon, sausage, ham, salami):** Instead, use legumes, nuts, seeds and either seafood, poultry or eggs.
- **Fried food and processed food:** These may contain poor fats, such as trans fats and saturated fats. Use olive oil to shallow fry at home, but don't allow it to smoke, as the beneficial nutrients and phytochemicals are destroyed when the oil is overheated. In fact, overheating creates harmful free radicals.

Lifestyle

It wasn't just what the Greeks and southern Italians ate prior to 1960 that kept them living long, disease-free lives. Equally significant was *how* they lived. We can learn from their:

- **Pace of life:** Life in rural villages moved at a gentle tempo. There were no lengthy commutes and no continuous streams of emails and communications. People had great support from their larger families and close communities. They ate long, leisurely meals together. We need to find a better way to manage modern technology or it will continue to disconnect us from our families and friends. Put away phones and screens where possible, especially at the table.
- **Active life:** Southern Greece and Crete consisted mostly of small towns and agricultural communities. Physical activity was a routine part of people's lives. We certainly don't do the heavy lifting that was typical of farm life then, but we can dress for the weather and get regular exercise as families.
- **Outdoor life:** People spent a lot of time outdoors in the sun, enabling their bodies to make vitamin D, which boosted immunity and protected against disease. Today people wear more protective sunscreen and need to regularly check their vitamin D levels.

Getting started with the Mediterranean Mood Food Plan

Of course, it's not possible to find pre-1960s Greek ingredients in supermarkets today, but we can choose similar nutritious foods. Here are some items that should be part of your regular meals.

- **Fish and seafood:** Oily fish includes salmon, tuna, mackerel, trout, herring and sardines. Seafood includes clams, mussels, prawns, crab, white fish and all types of seaweed. Seafood is an excellent source of selenium, zinc and other minerals.
- **Fresh, seasonal vegetables, fruits and herbs:** Eat a wide variety of veg, such as asparagus, beetroot, green and other bell peppers, broccoli, red and green cabbage, carrots, celery, avocados, cucumbers, aubergines, fennel, green beans, leafy green vegetables, lettuce, mushrooms, onions, peas, potatoes, radishes, butternut squash, tomatoes and okra.
- **Jars of artichokes, olives and pickles:** These are handy for snacks or enhancing your dishes.
- **Flavour your water:** Add herbs and whole fruits to table jugs and sports bottles. Try combinations such as blackberry and sage, strawberries and mint, or orange slices and rosemary.

- **Local farmhouse cheeses and natural and Greek yogurt:** The craft of cheese making is determined by the type of milk (goat, cow or ewe), the pasture where the animal grazed, the climate and the time of year. Great cheese is made with the best raw materials. Avoid yogurts with added sugar. Sweeten natural and Greek yogurts with chopped fruit and a little local honey.
- **Organic, enriched or free-range eggs:** Organic eggs come from chickens that are not treated with hormones and that eat an organic feed. Enriched eggs come from chickens that are given a conventional feed supplemented with a food rich in omega-3, such as linseeds. Supermarket free-range eggs come from chickens that are allowed to roam around and pick at insects and are also given a commercial feed. Choose the best eggs your budget allows.
- **Dried and tinned pulses, nuts and seeds:** Eat a variety of black-eyed peas, chickpeas, kidney beans, lentils, butter beans, cannellini beans, almonds, cashews, pine nuts, peanuts, hazelnuts, walnuts, pistachios, Brazil nuts, linseeds, poppy seeds, chia seeds, pumpkin seeds, sesame seeds and sunflower seeds.
- **Whole grains and high-fibre carbs:** Try something new occasionally, such as farro, wild rice, barley, buckwheat, bulgur wheat, kamut, steel cut oats, quinoa, 100% wholewheat flour or 100% sourdough breads or rolls.
- **Olives and olive oil:** Use a standard olive oil for cooking and extra virgin olive oil for your dressings and dips. The deeper the colour of the olive oil, the higher the polyphenol content (polyphenols benefit the body and help to fight disease). Extra virgin olive oil is ideal in salad dressings or for dipping a little crusty bread in. Rapeseed, grapeseed and camelina oil are also good choices.
- **Herbs and spices:** Oregano and rosemary are two of the most popular Greek herbs. Greeks often use these herbs and cinnamon to flavour lamb. Have a good selection of the following fresh or dried herbs and spices on hand: basil, chilli/chilli flakes, cloves, cumin, dill, garlic, ginger, fennel seed, marjoram, mint, nutmeg, oregano, parsley, pepper, saffron, sage, tarragon and thyme.
- **Vinegar:** Popular vinegars include balsamic, red wine, white wine and apple cider vinegar. Mix with some olive oil to make a salad dressing. Add oregano, garlic and mustard for extra flavour.

What else can you do?

Review your stock of herbs and spices

Apparently, there are millions of euro worth of unused herbs and spices languishing in forgotten corners of our kitchens. Take some time to review your stock. Many of us own jars of spices that are more than five years out of date. Some might be older than your children! Most ground spices diminish in flavour after six months, but whole spices can last up to a few years. Use whole spices where possible and grind them yourself in a coffee grinder or with a pestle and mortar. Store in airtight containers.

When reviewing your spice rack, you could do one of the following:

- Throw them out, especially if they haven't been stored correctly or if they are well past their best-by date, as they really won't add much sparkle to your meals.
- Make a spicy stock mix or paste and freeze it in ice cube trays as a great base for a quick curry. You can supplement and enhance the flavour with a fresh herb or spice.
- Make a herb- or spice-infused oil (which also freezes well) for quick meals.

Review your stock of nuts and seeds

Aflatoxins are poisonous human carcinogens and are regularly found in out-of-date seeds, peanuts and tree nuts or ones that have been poorly stored in unsealed containers or in damp, moist conditions. Throw out any old stock and only buy small quantities from trusted brands that comply with food regulations or ask your supplier about their aflatoxin control procedures.

Nut and seeds mixes are a nutritious and affordable snack that tick all the nutrition boxes. They contain mostly unsaturated healthy fats, protein and fibre, plus they're tasty and satisfying. They contain a myriad of vitamins, minerals and phytonutrients, with no added sugar. In old times walnuts and other tree nuts were simply plucked from the trees as an ideal snack. Today you can buy unsalted versions, which are certainly a good alternative provided you stick to a handful approximately four times a week.

Review your stock of oils

Pare back on the number of oils you use. Technically, any oil can go rancid. If an open bottle of oil has been sitting in sunlight on your kitchen countertop for over six months, it's probably best to jettison it. Pour a little oil onto your fingers and check its tackiness – if it feels sticky, get rid of it. Oxygen, enzymes and heat all contribute to rancidity and vegetable and olive oils are particularly susceptible.

If an oil has already been subjected to heat (e.g. toasted sesame oil), store it in the fridge when not in regular use. Traditional Mediterranean olive oils were probably used within a year of harvest. Today, unopened olive oil (stored in a cool dark place) will be good for up to two years. After that, the quality will gradually decline. Extra virgin oils are greener in colour and hardier. These polyphenol-rich oils are also more peppery and bitter and are great for salad dressings. They will keep longer than delicate ripe ones, which you should use quickly (ideally within six months).

Prepare

When you're on the move and time poor, spend two hours on Sunday shopping and chopping. You can make up to five desk-fast breakfasts and lunchtime salad jars in less than an hour once you have all the ingredients at your fingertips. Transport your meals in glass containers with tight-fitting lids (e.g. Kilner jars). Get online or down to your local home store to stockpile jars, water bottles, travel mugs and luncheon-ware. It's not about being hipster – it's about being prepared to save you precious time.

If making a salad in a jar, always put the dressing in first, at the bottom of the jar, so it can't make your lunch greens soggy. Layering your ingredients in the jar means they never touch until you're ready to shake them up together and it all stays nice and crisp in the meantime. I love the way they can last for up to five days, meaning you can just grab one on the way out to work.

For breakfast on the move, make a large bowl of chia seed mix (see the recipe on page 59). Divide it between your jars and top with various chopped fresh fruits, stewed fruits, nuts and seeds for a grab-and-go option.

Drink more water

Hydration is key for performance. Unfortunately, certain commercial flavoured waters can have similar amounts of sugar as soft drinks, so it's best to make your own. Plain tap water has no calories, no sugar to cause weight gain and tooth decay, no carbonation or citric acid to erode teeth enamel and no preservatives or colours. It's the best rehydrating agent around. If you really need to jazz up the flavour of water, all you need is a water bottle with an infuser to introduce a hint of flavour. This type of bottle features a hollow screw-on section that holds your fruits or herbs so that their flavour infuses into your water but it's all kept nice and tidy inside the tube. These water bottles usually have a handle and flip-top closure. Add your own ingredients and off you go! Here are some ideas to get you started:

- **Blackberries and sage:** Lightly crush a sprig of sage with your fingers and add to the infuser. Throw in a few crushed blackberries on top.
- **Peach and mint:** Add an entire sprig of mint and some gently crushed peach flesh.
- **Citrus melody:** Slice one orange, one lime and one lemon into rounds, then cut the slices in half, keeping the skin on the flesh. Add to your infuser, squeezing some of the juice gently into the bottle.
- **Raspberry and lime:** Slice one lime into rounds, then cut the slices in half. Squeeze some of the juice into the bottle, then place slices in the infuser and throw in some raspberries on top. pressing them gently.

Manage your mind

It's easy to have unhelpful thoughts about food, such as 'I'd prefer to cut my leg off than eat an olive!' Repeat a thought often enough and it becomes a certainty. Beliefs held over time can become entrenched and difficult to budge. If you don't like olives, could you be open to the possibility that you might someday if you keep trying? You can learn to like new foods – it's a learned response. Taste olives often enough and the taste becomes familiar. It can even be a pleasant experience in time. Frequently taste, and adaptation follows. Be open to change.

Try to adhere to the 10 pillars of the MMFP as best you can. You don't have to eat perfectly all the time – allow yourself the odd treat or peccadillo! However, that's not to suggest you should let yourself off the hook too frequently. You won't get the benefits by following a watered-down version of the plan.

The recipes

I'm a dietitian, not a chef. Although I love my food, I'm always looking for nutritious, simple dishes to put together without fuss, so you won't find recipes here that require any great culinary skills. The recipes are simple and straightforward – the intention is that you can throw a dish together with whatever you happen to have in the fridge. The ingredients for the most part are accessible and affordable. Just compare your monthly food bills to the cost of cosmetics for your hair, skin and nails!

You can build up your own recipe collection to complement the 10 pillars of the MMFP. The burgeoning bank of recipes online can inspire your MMFP so that it never gets boring. The recipes in this book have been adapted from and inspired by a number of great chefs I have had the privilege to know and work with in Ireland and the UK.

So refresh your routine and reset the table, choosing from over 80 meal solutions. I hope you find the recipes appetising and flavoursome. The more you adhere to this way of eating, the greater the benefits for your body and brain.

The 10 pillars of the MMFP

Eat more
vegetables and
fruit

Eat more
olive oil

Eat more legumes,
nuts and seeds

Eat more
oily fish

Eat more herbs, spices and seaweed

Eat up to seven eggs per week

Eat moderate amounts of whole grains (more if you are active)

Eat less red meat and processed meat

Eat moderate amounts of probiotic foods

Eat less processed, refined carbs and sugars

Breakfast

Banana and passion fruit chia pots

A tart passion fruit is a beautiful thing, especially when combined with a sweet ripe banana. It's a wonderful fruit combo, high in potassium, fibre and vitamin C. Bananas are a great prebiotic food that selectively feed the good gut bacteria and promote a healthy gut–brain axis.

Serves 2

500ml cow's or almond milk

4 heaped tbsp chia seeds

2 tsp honey

1 tsp vanilla extract

2 ripe bananas, sliced

2 passion fruit

2 tbsp toasted or plain flaked almonds

Stir together the milk, chia seeds, honey and vanilla extract. Let sit for 15 minutes or while you shower. Once the chia seeds have plumped up, stir it up and divide between two breakfast pots.

Cover each pot with the sliced bananas. Cut the passion fruit in half and use a spoon to scoop out the seeds and fruit over the banana, then top with the almonds.

If you are on the move, put the chia mixture into two jars that have tight-fitting lids and keep upright if possible.

Apricot and walnut steel cut oatmeal

Nothing beats a good bowl of stirabout. Oats are super versatile whole grains that are low in saturated fat and high in gut-protective soluble fibre. Oats contain no added sugar or salt, so you can dress them up with some natural sweetness, such as dried apricots or a fruit of your choice. Walnuts make a nice brain-sustaining topping that's rich in omega-3, but you can use macadamia nuts, linseeds or chia seeds too.

Serves 2

100g Irish steel cut porridge oats (or any porridge oats you like)

4 dried apricots, chopped (or 2 chopped plums or 1 chopped nectarine), plus extra to serve

100ml cow's or almond milk

100ml or so of water, to your liking

Drizzle of natural or Greek yogurt

Drizzle of local honey

2 tbsp chopped walnuts

Soak the steel cut oats and dried apricots overnight in the milk and water.

Heat and divide between two bowls the following morning. Drizzle with a little natural or Greek yogurt and local honey, then scatter over the walnuts and extra chopped dried apricots.

Turmeric porridge

This might be a step too far for some, but this colourful porridge can put a smile on your face as you start your day. The wholegrain oats feed the good gut bacteria and help to prevent dysbiosis (a microbial imbalance), thus maintaining good brain function. A morning bowl of beta-glucan-rich porridge can benefit your heart health too by lowering your cholesterol. Turmeric has many antioxidant and anti-inflammatory compounds, including curcumin. Older people in India who regularly eat turmeric have the lowest rates of Alzheimer's disease in the world.

Serves 2

100g Irish steel cut porridge oats (or any porridge oats you like)

200ml cow's or almond milk

1–2 tsp ground turmeric or 1 x 2.5cm piece of fresh turmeric

1 tsp ground cinnamon

2 tbsp raspberries

2 tsp mixed seeds

Sprinkle of toasted flaked almonds

Drizzle of local honey, to serve (optional)

Chopped fresh fruit, to serve (optional)

Soak the oats in cold water overnight. Drain off the water in the morning.

Put your oats in a saucepan with the milk, turmeric and cinnamon. Cook over a medium heat for up to 10 minutes, until the oats are cooked and creamy.

Divide between two bowls and top each bowl with the raspberries, mixed seeds and toasted flaked almonds. If you need to sweeten your porridge, add a drizzle of local honey or some chopped fresh fruit.

Spicy compote for your porridge

I simply love cinnamon. It's one of the spices that makes the winter bearable. This warm spicy compote will dress up your porridge and get your taste buds zinging, no matter what the weather! Cinnamon, like many spices, has antioxidant and anti-inflammatory properties. Including cinnamon, cloves, nutmeg, ginger and cardamom regularly in freshly made meals has been shown in recent studies to improve memory, increase attention span and enhance cognitive processing.

**Makes about
12 tablespoons**

55g dried cherries

55g dried blueberries

55g dried figs

55g dried jumbo
sultanas or raisins

55g dried mango

5 cloves

1 cinnamon stick

½ vanilla pod, cut in half
lengthways

1 tbsp local honey

Zest of 1 lemon
(optional)

Toasted flaked almonds,
for sprinkling (optional)

Toasted pine nuts, for
sprinkling (optional)

Place all the dried fruit in a saucepan and cover with cold water. Pop in the cloves, cinnamon stick, vanilla, local honey and lemon zest. You can use any other dried fruit that you like, such as apricots, apples or other berries.

Bring gently to the boil, then reduce the heat, cover the saucepan and simmer for about 15 minutes. Check on it every so often and add some more water if you need to.

Remove the cloves and cinnamon stick, then pour the compote into a clean jar with an airtight lid. The compote will keep in the fridge for about a week – if it lasts that long! This is delicious with overnight oats, over porridge or with natural yogurt. Sprinkle some toasted flaked almonds and toasted pine nuts on top for a little added texture and nuttiness.

Sourdough, avocado and feta doorsteps

This is one of my all-time favourites. My fetish for sourdough bread drizzled with extra virgin olive oil and rubbed with garlic started on a skiing trip. I love it topped with grilled mixed mushrooms, but tomato and basil are great too. When I don't have fresh basil, chilli flakes are my go-to. Avocados are rich in good monounsaturated fat, which supports the production of acetylcholine, the memory and learning brain chemical. A good balance of fats (with more unsaturated fat and less processed trans and saturated fat) promotes a healthy blood flow to the brain.

Serves 2

½ large or 1 small avocado

Squeeze of lime or lemon juice

Drizzle of extra virgin olive oil (optional)

1 garlic clove, halved (optional)

2 thick slices of sourdough or 100% wholegrain bread, lightly toasted

2 ripe tomatoes, finely chopped

2 matchbox-sized pieces of feta cheese, crumbled

A few fresh basil leaves, shredded

Lots of freshly ground black pepper

Chilli flakes (optional)

Coarsely mash the avocado with the lime or lemon juice on a plate.

Brush a little extra virgin olive oil onto the bread, then rub with a halved garlic clove if you like.

Spread the mashed avocado on the heated bread, then top with the chopped tomatoes, crumbled feta and basil.

Get your black pepper and chilli flake grinders and season to your taste.

Spinach, feta and egg bake

A handy little brunch for the weekend, this egg bake is a great way to use up any leftover roasted vegetables, sweet potatoes, beans or cheese ends. You can make it in one ovenproof dish if you haven't got individual ones. Olives contain a phenolic compound called oleocanthal that has strong anti-inflammatory properties. The olives also contain essential omega-3 fatty acids, which our bodies can't make so we need to eat them. Luckily, olives are a delicious way to include omega-3 in recipes.

Serves 4

100g spinach

1 x 400g tin of chopped tomatoes

100g feta cheese, cubed

10 pitted black olives, sliced (optional)

2 garlic cloves, crushed

1 tsp chilli flakes

1 tsp dried oregano

Lots of freshly ground black pepper

4 eggs

Toasted sourdough bread, to serve

Garlic-infused olive oil, to serve

Preheat the oven to 180°C.

Place the spinach in a colander set in the sink and pour a kettle of boiling water over it. Squeeze the excess water out of the wilted leaves, then divide it between four small individual ovenproof dishes.

Put the tomatoes, feta, olives (if using), garlic, chilli flakes, oregano and seasoning in a bowl and mix it all up, then add to the dishes with the spinach. Make a well in the centre of each and crack in an egg.

Bake in the oven for 15 minutes or more, until the eggs are cooked to your liking.

Serve with sourdough toast brushed with garlic-infused olive oil.

Lunch

Butter bean, garlic and dill dip

These high-fibre dips are handy for family snacks and weekend nibbles.

Serves 4

1 x 400g tin of butter beans, drained and rinsed

125g natural yogurt

50g crème fraîche

50ml extra virgin olive oil

Juice of ½ lemon

2 garlic cloves, crushed

Chopped fresh dill

Salt and freshly ground black pepper

Blitz all the ingredients together in a blender or food processor. Serve with your favourite wholegrain crackers or toasted pitta bread soldiers.

Artichoke and olive dip

Artichokes, a wonderful prebiotic vegetable, provide fuel that good gut bacteria thrive on. If they are fermented, they also contain healthy probiotic bacteria. When eaten regularly, the transient probiotics in fermented vegetables encourage a healthy balance of bacteria in the gut microbiome.

Serves 6

1 jar of chargrilled artichokes in oil

1 jar of pitted green olives

50g Parmesan cheese, finely grated

30g pine nuts

Juice of ½ lemon

Wholegrain sourdough toast, to serve

Drain the jar of artichokes and set aside 2 tablespoons of the oil to use later. Set aside two olives and chop into quarters.

Throw the rest of the olives and all the artichokes into a food processer along with the Parmesan, pine nuts and lemon juice and blend to a paste. Mix in the reserved oil, then spoon into a serving bowl.

Garnish with the chopped olives. Serve at room temperature with torn pieces of wholegrain sourdough toast about an hour after making the dip so that the flavour has fully developed.

Aubergine and yogurt dip

Aubergines have a vibrant purple colour because of anthocyanins in the skin. One of these anthocyanins is called nasunin. It's a potent antioxidant and free radical scavenger. Nasunin helps to protect cell membranes in our brains, which are mostly made up of lipids. This lipid layer helps the brain cell to let nutrients in, let waste out and receive messages that help the cell to function well.

Serves 4

2 large aubergines

2 garlic cloves, crushed

1 tbsp extra virgin olive oil

1 tbsp lemon juice

190g drained roasted red peppers from a jar, finely diced

150ml natural yogurt

Salt and freshly ground black pepper

25g pitted black olives, chopped

1 green pepper, deseeded and cut into strips, to serve

150g celery, cut into sticks, to serve

125g carrots, peeled and cut into 5cm batons, to serve

Preheat the oven to 200°C.

Pierce the skin of the aubergines with a fork and place on a baking tray. Cook in the oven for 40 minutes, until very soft. Allow to cool, then cut in half and scoop out the flesh into a bowl.

Mash the aubergines with the garlic, olive oil and lemon juice until smooth or blend for a few seconds in a food processor.

Add the chopped peppers to the aubergine mixture, then stir in the yogurt. Season to taste with salt and pepper, then add the chopped black olives. Put in the fridge to chill for at least 30 minutes.

Put the green pepper, celery and carrot strips on a plate and serve as crudités to accompany the dip.

Hummus

Hummus is naturally high in healthy unsaturated fat because of the olive oil and the sesame seeds in the tahini. Hummus is also a pretty good source of plant-based protein and fibre. Instead of adding lots of salt, you can flavour it with chilli flakes, or try adding caramelised or roasted vegetables.

Serves 4

1 x 400g tin of chickpeas, drained and rinsed

1 garlic clove, crushed

2 tbsp tahini

Juice of 1 lemon

1 tsp ground cumin

Salt and freshly ground black pepper

Extra virgin olive oil

Toasted pitta bread soldiers or carrot and cucumber sticks, to serve

Put the drained chickpeas, garlic, tahini and lemon juice in a food processor and blend until smooth. If it's very thick add some cooled boiled water to thin the consistency, but it should be thick and creamy. Season with the cumin and some salt and pepper.

Blend again and taste. Add more of anything if you feel it needs it, but no one flavour should dominate. Transfer to a bowl and cover with a thin film of olive oil. It's best to leave it for an hour or two so that the flavours can develop.

Serve at room temperature with toasted pitta bread soldiers or carrot and cucumber sticks for dipping.

Toast with smoked salmon pâté and Kalamata olives

Kalamata olives are large black or brown olives with a smooth, meaty texture, named after the city of Kalamata in the southern Peloponnese in Greece. The olives themselves contain good fibre, essential anti-inflammatory omega-3 fatty acids and few calories. Oil made from these olives can contain over 30 phenolic compounds that are potent antioxidants and free radical scavengers. These protect the brain and tissues in the body.

Serves 4

200g soft sheep's or goat's cheese

100g crème fraîche

100g smoked salmon

Zest and juice of 1 lemon

Pinch of cracked black pepper

Pinch of chilli flakes

Drizzle of extra virgin olive oil, to serve

Wholegrain sourdough bread or pitta bread, to serve

Pitted black Kalamata olives, sliced, to serve

Put the soft cheese, crème fraîche, smoked salmon and lemon zest and juice into a food processor. Whizz until smooth, then stir in a very large pinch of cracked black pepper and some chilli flakes.

Spoon the mix into a serving bowl and drizzle with extra virgin olive oil. Serve with toasted wholegrain sourdough or pitta bread and sliced Kalamata olives.

LUNCH

Courgette and goat's cheese omelette

Many of us can enjoy eggs despite the fact that they contain dietary cholesterol, as it has very little effect on our blood cholesterol levels. Chemically processed fat, such as trans fat, and certain saturated fats, however, do impact badly on our blood cholesterol levels and on the blood flow to the brain and around the body. Eggs are a source of choline, a precursor of another important brain nutrient, citicoline. Citicoline helps increase the blood flow to the brain and enhances its ability to utilise glucose, which is the primary fuel for the brain.

Serves 2

1 tbsp olive oil, plus an extra drizzle to serve

1 small courgette per person, grated

1 garlic clove, crushed

Salt and freshly ground black pepper

4 eggs

50g goat's cheese, crumbled

A handful of chopped fresh dill

A handful of spinach, to serve

Heat ½ tablespoon of the oil in a non-stick ovenproof pan over a medium heat. Add the grated courgette and cook for about 2 minutes. Stir in the garlic and cook for another minute. Season to taste with salt and pepper, then remove from the heat.

Beat the eggs in a large bowl with the goat's cheese. Add a little more salt and pepper, then stir in the courgette and dill.

Clean and dry the pan, then return to a medium-high heat and add the remaining olive oil. When hot, pour in half the egg mixture per person, tilting the pan to distribute the eggs and filling. During the first few minutes of cooking, shake the pan gently and tilt it slightly, then use a spatula to lift an edge and let the uncooked eggs run underneath.

Turn the heat to low, cover the pan and cook for 2 to 3 minutes, shaking the pan gently now and then, until the bottom is golden.

Meanwhile, turn on the grill.

Uncover the pan and place under the grill, not too close to the heat, for 1 to 3 minutes, making sure it doesn't burn.

Allow to cool for 2 minutes, then loosen the edges. Carefully slide from the pan onto a dinner plate. Fold the omelette and dress with spinach leaves and your favourite salad.

Pesto potato frittata

Eggs are high in the amino acid tryptophan, which helps to produce the neurotransmitter serotonin, aka the happy hormone. Eggs are also a good source of choline, which is a precursor of acetylcholine, a neurotransmitter important for learning and memory. Enjoy an egg a day or include them in dishes three times a week. Eggs and cheese provide the protein in this recipe and you can always add a few chopped nuts too for texture. Top the frittata with peppery rocket and serve with a tomato and basil salad.

Serves 4

4 potatoes, unpeeled and thinly sliced

2 garlic cloves, finely chopped

Salt and freshly ground black pepper

8 large eggs, lightly beaten

1 tbsp olive oil

100g soft goat's cheese

2 large handfuls of rocket

4 dessertspoons pesto

Boil the potato slices in salted water for 5 minutes, until just tender.

Meanwhile, preheat the oven to 220°C.

Add the garlic and seasoning to the lightly beaten eggs in a large bowl. Drain the potatoes, then stir them into the egg mix.

Heat the oil in an ovenproof frying pan, then pour in the egg and potato mixture. Cook over a low heat for 5 minutes, until the frittata is almost fully set, then pop the pan in the oven for 10 minutes to cook completely. Dot the soft goat's cheese on top of the frittata for the last minute.

Slide the frittata out of the pan, then cut into wedges. To serve, place a small handful of rocket on each slice, then drizzle with a dessertspoon of pesto.

Sweet potato frittata

Reducing salt and alcohol intake is beneficial for blood pressure management. However, increasing potassium intake may be just as important as keeping the sodium (salt) down in the foods we eat. Seventy per cent of the salt we eat comes in processed food, so when we cut these foods to a minimum, our salt intake drops dramatically. According to a National Health and Nutrition Examination survey, less than 5% of American adults are meeting the daily recommendation for potassium. Eating approximately seven portions of fruit and veg per day can really increase your potassium levels and sweet potato is a great source.

Serves 2

2 sweet potatoes, peeled and cut into cubes

1 litre vegetable stock

A splash of olive oil

2 red peppers, deseeded and finely chopped

1 small red onion, finely chopped

1 garlic clove, finely chopped

1 sprig of fresh rosemary, finely chopped

1 tsp ground nutmeg

A large handful of rocket, chopped

3 medium eggs

2 tbsp milk

Oil a 20cm round cake tin (or if it's non-stick, line it with non-stick baking paper).

Boil the sweet potatoes in the stock for 10 minutes, until soft, then drain and roughly mash with a fork.

Heat the olive oil in a non-stick frying pan over a medium heat. Add the peppers, onion, garlic, rosemary and nutmeg. Cook until the onions are soft, then add the mashed sweet potatoes and rocket. Remove from the heat.

Whisk together the eggs and milk, then add the potato mixture and pour it all into the cake tin. Bake in the oven for 15 minutes, then take it out and gently but firmly pat down the mixture to help make it solid. Put it back in the oven for another 15 minutes. It may well rise in the centre from time to time, but will sink down when it cools.

Cut into wedges and serve with a grilled tuna steak. It's delicious hot or cold and is a great addition to lunchboxes.

Minted courgettes

Both courgettes and mint are easy to grow, making this a simple garden-fresh salad that you can rustle up in minutes. Courgettes contain potassium, which is key to controlling blood pressure. The soluble fibre in the skin slows down digestion and consequently helps to stabilise blood glucose and insulin levels.

Serves 4

½ red onion, thinly sliced

Zest and juice of 1 lemon

Salt and freshly ground black pepper

2 courgettes

2 tbsp extra virgin olive oil

A large handful of fresh mint leaves, roughly torn

Mix the onion and lemon juice together with some seasoning and set aside to marinate.

Grab a vegetable peeler to thinly slice the courgettes into ribbons. Place the ribbons in a serving bowl with the onion and lemon juice, then add the olive oil, lemon zest and mint. Gently toss together and serve straight away.

LUNCH

Vegetable and lentil soup

Lentils are a high-protein, high-fibre member of the legume family. Like a mini version of a bean, lentils grow in pods and come in red, brown, black and green varieties. They are relatively inexpensive, quick and easy to prepare compared to dried beans and they don't have to be soaked overnight. Lentils are a good natural source of selenium and folate, which are important nutrients for brain health.

Serves 2

1 onion

2 large carrots

2 celery sticks

1 large courgette

1 red pepper

2 garlic cloves

1 tbsp olive oil

1 litre vegetable stock

50g dried red lentils

Freshly ground black pepper

Chopped fresh parsley, to garnish

Chop all the vegetables into similar small bite-sized pieces and crush the garlic cloves.

Heat the oil in a large saucepan over a medium heat. Add the onion and garlic and cook until softened. Add the rest of the vegetables and stir well to coat with the oil.

Add the stock and bring to the boil, then reduce the heat and simmer for about 20 minutes, until all the vegetables have softened. Meanwhile, rinse the lentils in a sieve.

When the vegetables are almost cooked, add the lentils and cook for a further 15 minutes.

Blend half or all of the soup with a hand-held blender or in a food processor. Season to taste with freshly ground black pepper. Serve piping hot in your favourite mug and garnish with chopped fresh parsley.

Sourdough bread salad

Although a good fermented sourdough starter contains gut-friendly *Lactobacilli*, the baked sourdough bread does not because the heat of the baking process destroys them. I include sourdough bread in these recipes because it tastes great and is more in line with how we traditionally enjoyed baked bread, plus a 100% wholewheat sourdough provides a lot of fibre.

Serves 4

400g sourdough bread, preferably a bit stale (if not, dry it out in a low oven for a while)

1 garlic clove

1 medium red onion, thinly sliced

400g tomatoes, peeled and cut into wedges

4 tbsp extra virgin olive oil

2 tbsp green olives stuffed with anchovies, roughly chopped

1½ tbsp capers

1½ tbsp red wine vinegar

Salt and freshly ground black pepper

A few sprigs of fresh oregano, leaves removed from the stalks and roughly chopped

Tiny fresh basil leaves, to garnish

Green salad, to serve (optional)

Mature cheese, to serve (optional)

Slice the bread into thick pieces and cut the garlic clove in half. Rub each piece of bread on both sides with the halved garlic clove, then tear the bread into bitesized pieces. Set aside.

Mix the onion with the tomatoes, oil, olives, capers and red wine vinegar and season to taste. Leave to stand for 30–60 minutes at room temperature. Throw in the bread pieces and oregano just before serving and mix well. Taste again and adjust the seasoning if necessary.

Garnish with a few tiny basil leaves. Serve with a green salad and some mature cheese if you like.

Greek salad

There's nothing as delicious as a Greek salad eaten outdoors in the sun. Herbs such as oregano, which has been cultivated for centuries in the Mediterranean, are key. *Origanum vulgare*, also referred to as Spanish thyme and wild marjoram, is widely available. Medicinal uses date back to the ancient Greek and Roman empires. The leaves were used to treat skin sores, relieve aching muscles and as an antiseptic. Oregano oils contain several antioxidants and anti-inflammatory properties.

Serves 4

4 large handfuls of romaine lettuce, torn or sliced

A handful of purslane, rocket or watercress, torn or chopped

16 thick slices of English cucumber

16 cherry tomatoes, halved

16 pitted Kalamata olives, halved

1 red onion, thinly sliced

1 red pepper, deseeded and sliced

100g feta or goat's cheese (optional)

2 tsp fresh or dried oregano

1 tsp fresh or dried basil

4 tbsp extra virgin olive oil

3 tbsp balsamic or red wine vinegar

1 tbsp freshly squeezed lemon juice

Put all the salad ingredients except for the oregano and basil in a large salad bowl and toss to combine.

Just before serving, sprinkle on the oregano and basil. Pour the olive oil over the salad, followed by the vinegar and lemon juice, and toss once more. Serve immediately.

Avocado and mixed bean salad with toasted sunflower seeds

Beans are rich in a type of antioxidant called polyphenols. Antioxidants fight the effects of free radicals, mopping them up with positive effects on a wide range of bodily functions, from physical and neurological ageing to managing the inflammatory process and reducing our risk of cancer.

Serves 4

60g sunflower seeds

250g mixed leaves

1 x 400g tin of mixed beans, drained and rinsed

1 packet of sprouts, such as alfalfa sprouts

3 spring onions, thinly sliced

2 avocados, halved, stoned, peeled and sliced

For the dressing:

4 tbsp extra virgin olive oil

1 tbsp sherry vinegar

1 tsp Dijon mustard

Small drizzle of local honey

Salt and freshly ground black pepper

Preheat the oven to 180°C.

Spread the sunflower seeds on a baking tray and toast them in the oven for 5–10 minutes.

To make the dressing, whisk together all the ingredients in a small bowl.

Put the salad leaves in a large bowl with the beans, sprouts, spring onions and avocados.

While the sunflower seeds are still hot, sprinkle them over the salad, then immediately pour over the dressing. Toss well, then transfer to a clean bowl to serve.

Cannellini bean salad with lemon and rocket

Known for its peppery taste, rocket is commonly used to intensify flavour in salads. Here, it packs a punch with the protein and fibre of the cannellini beans, the bite from the red onion and the hit of lemon from the homemade vinaigrette. Rocket – and all greens – are full of protective nutrients that are crucial for a healthy nervous system. Studies show that people who consume one to two servings of greens every day experience fewer memory problems and cognitive decline than people who rarely eat greens.

Serves 4

2 tbsp extra virgin olive oil

2 tbsp freshly squeezed lemon juice

1 tsp lemon zest

1 tsp Dijon mustard

Salt and freshly ground black pepper

1 x 400g tin of cannellini beans, drained and rinsed

1 red onion, thinly sliced

4 large handfuls of rocket

Combine the oil, lemon juice and zest, mustard and some salt and pepper in a large bowl, stirring with a whisk. Add the beans and onion and toss well to coat. Add the rocket and toss gently to combine.

Avocado, bean and cashew salad

This simple salad has fewer than 200 calories per portion and about 16g of fat, but the majority of it is healthy monounsaturated fat from the olives, nuts and avocados.

Serves 4

1 small cucumber, chopped into chunks

20 cherry tomatoes, halved

1 x 400g tin of mixed beans, drained and rinsed

A handful of mixed salad leaves

2 tbsp extra virgin olive oil

2 tbsp orange juice

2 avocados

20 raw cashew nuts

12 pitted black olives, halved

Mix the cucumber, tomatoes, beans and salad leaves together.

Put the olive oil and orange juice in a screw-top jar.

When you're ready to eat, shake the jar to combine the oil and juice, then pour over the vegetables and beans and toss.

Halve, stone, peel and dice the avocados and scatter over the top of the salad along with the cashews and olives. Toss and serve.

Broccoli, carrot and mixed seed salad

Pumpkin seeds and their oil contain the fat-soluble vitamin E. This vitamin acts like an antioxidant and can help to maintain healthy blood vessels. It also supports a healthy immune system.

Serves 4

2 tbsp mixed seeds (pumpkin, sunflower, sesame)

1 medium-sized head of broccoli

4 carrots, coarsely grated

Zest and juice of 1 orange

4 tbsp sesame oil

120g goat's cheese, crumbled (optional)

Preheat the oven to 180°C.

Spread the seeds on a baking tray and toast them in the oven for 5–10 minutes.

Wash the broccoli and divide into small, similar-sized florets. Combine in a bowl with the carrots, orange juice and zest and sesame oil. Sprinkle over the toasted mixed seeds.

Serve with 30g of your favourite goat's cheese per person if you like.

Butternut squash and Puy lentil salad with marinated feta

This makes a tasty lunch option. Tofu can be used instead of the marinated feta to make this dairy free. A portion of butternut squash contains about 3g of fibre and even more potassium than a banana. It's a very good source of antioxidants, vitamin C and beta-carotene, the precursor of vitamin A.

Serves 4

1 small or medium butternut squash

2 tsp olive oil, plus extra for greasing

2 tsp tamari or soy sauce

100g Puy lentils

200ml water

1 garlic clove, crushed

1 small bay leaf

1 tsp vegetable bouillon

½ tsp dried thyme

4 tbsp extra virgin olive oil

1 tbsp balsamic vinegar

1 heaped tsp Dijon mustard

1 tsp local honey

200g marinated feta cheese (page 97)

Preheat the oven to 200°C. Lightly oil a baking tray.

Cut the unpeeled butternut squash in half and scoop out the seeds. Place the squash on the baking tray, cut side up. Mix together the regular olive oil and tamari and liberally brush the cut side of the squash. Bake in the oven for 30–40 minutes, until tender. Set aside to cool.

Meanwhile, put the lentils in a sieve and hold under a running tap for a few seconds to rinse off any dust. Drain and place in a saucepan with the water, garlic, bay leaf, bouillon and thyme. Bring to the boil, then turn down to a simmer and cover the pan. Cook for 20–25 minutes, until the lentils are just tender.

When the squash is cool enough to handle, scoop out the flesh using a large spoon, then chop into small cubes and set aside. If the squash is large, you can keep the leftovers in the fridge and use it in a soup the next day.

When the lentils are cooked, drain off any remaining liquid and remove the bay leaf, then transfer to a large bowl.

Make the dressing by whisking the extra virgin olive oil, vinegar, mustard and honey together in a small bowl.

Add the butternut squash to the cooked lentils, then pour over the dressing and mix gently. Scatter the feta cheese over the salad and serve.

Marinated feta in thyme and chilli oil

Make a batch of this feta and the eight portions will keep in your fridge for a week. It's a fabulous shortcut to have on hand when you need to rustle up something quick, like an omelette. Olive oil is an integral part of the TMD. It has significant amounts of vitamins E and K, both of which are important for memory and maintaining good mental health. Olive oil raises levels of brain-derived neurotrophic factor, which supports the survival of existing neurons and cognitive function.

Serves 8

100ml olive oil

2 tbsp fresh thyme leaves, plus extra

4 garlic cloves, sliced

½ tsp chilli flakes

Freshly ground black pepper

2 x 200g packs of feta cheese

1 x 175g jar of artichoke hearts in oil

140g semi-sun-dried tomatoes in olive oil, drained

A handful of pitted Kalamata olives

Put the olive oil and thyme in a bowl and blitz with a hand-held blender. Stir in the garlic, chilli flakes and lots of black pepper. (You don't need any salt in this recipe.) Add a little oil from the jar of artichokes or tomatoes.

Pat dry and cut each block of feta into small cubes and arrange in a dish or food container with the artichokes, tomatoes and olives. Spoon over the herby oil, scatter with some extra thyme leaves and leave to marinate in the fridge until you need it.

Marinated feta with herbes de Provence, thyme and chilli

This can be used as part of the butternut squash and Puy lentil salad on page 94 or as part of a mezze platter.

Serves 8

1 x 200g packet of feta cheese

½ tsp dried herbes de Provence

½ tsp dried thyme

¼ tsp chilli flakes

3 tbsp extra virgin olive oil

Open the packet of cheese, drain and rinse. Pat the cheese dry with kitchen paper, then cut into small cubes. Put in a bowl and sprinkle over the herbs and chilli flakes. Pour over the oil and gently mix to coat.

Store in a covered bowl or sealed container and use within four days.

Beetroot, basil and toasted hazelnut salad

Beetroot is not just a favourite of athletes. This underrated vegetable is an acquired taste, but it's a nutritional powerhouse. Beetroot juice may help to increase blood flow to the ageing brain and help in the fight against dementia, according to a study in 2010. Beetroot also contains folate, which may help to prevent damage to the hippocampus, the part of the brain responsible for memory and learning.

Serves 4

50g blanched whole hazelnuts

4 tbsp extra virgin olive oil

1 tbsp balsamic vinegar

1 garlic clove, crushed

1 tsp Dijon mustard

1 tsp honey

6 small or medium cooked beetroot, cut into small chunks

1 small red onion, finely diced

2 celery sticks, thinly sliced

10 large fresh basil leaves, shredded, plus 1–2 leaves to garnish

A few teaspoons of soft goat's cheese (optional)

A handful of salad leaves (optional)

Gently toast the hazelnuts in a small dry frying pan over a medium heat. Tip out onto a plate and set aside to cool.

Make the dressing by whisking together the oil, vinegar, garlic, mustard and honey in a small bowl.

Put the beetroot in a medium-sized bowl with the onion, celery and basil.

Crush the cooled hazelnuts a little by putting them between two sheets of kitchen paper and pressing a rolling pin over them. Add to the beetroot.

Pour on the dressing and stir well, then spoon into a serving dish. Mix in some salad leaves and dot over a few teaspoons of soft goat's cheese if you like. Garnish with a basil leaf or two and serve.

Quick tuna salad

Oily fish is really a top-notch brain food. It's an excellent source of protein and contains all the essential amino acids necessary to produce mood-boosting neurotransmitters such as serotonin and dopamine. It also contains vitamin B12, an essential vitamin for a healthy brain and nervous system. Tuna is also a fantastic source of omega-3 fatty acids, a critical nutrient for brain health.

Serves 2

1 x 185g tin of dry tuna

1 orange, peeled, segmented and finely chopped

1 heaped dessertspoon natural yogurt

1 heaped dessertspoon crème fraîche

1 tbsp chopped cashews

1 tsp ground ginger

1 tsp lemon juice

Salt and freshly ground black pepper

Put all the ingredients in a medium bowl and mix well to combine. Serve over a bed of spinach or lettuce leaves and eat with a crusty, nutty wholemeal sourdough bread or pitta pockets.

Quinoa tabbouleh in lettuce cups

Tomatoes are a particularly good source of lycopene and beta-carotene. Like all carotenoids, these are powerful antioxidants. The brain, with its high content of omega-3 fatty acids, is vulnerable to attack from free radicals, but these carotenoids help to eliminate them and avoid inflammation. This is why we all need to eat more nutrient-rich fruit and vegetables. Studies have found that individuals with mild cognitive impairment as well as Alzheimer's disease have lower levels of carotenoids such as lycopene in their blood.

Serves 4

100g quinoa

400g cherry tomatoes (mixed colours if possible), halved

8 spring onions, thinly sliced

2 bunches of fresh flat-leaf parsley, chopped

1 bunch of fresh mint, chopped

1 Cos or 2 Little Gem lettuces

For the dressing:

Juice of 1 lemon

3–4 tbsp extra virgin olive oil

½ tsp ground cinnamon

¼ tsp ground allspice

Salt and freshly ground black pepper

Rinse the quinoa, then cook it in boiling water until tender. Drain well, then spread it out in a wide, shallow bowl or plate and stir through all the dressing ingredients. Leave to cool.

Add the cherry tomatoes to the cooled quinoa and stir through. Leave to stand for a couple of minutes.

Add the spring onions and herbs to the quinoa and tomatoes and mix well. Season to taste with salt and pepper.

Separate the leaves of the lettuce. Wash and dry them well. Serve the tabbouleh in the lettuce cups as a starter or as part of a mezze platter.

LUNCH

Chicken and grape salad

Scientists believe that grapes might support brain health by reducing oxidative stress in the brain and promoting healthy brain blood flow. A University of Los Angeles study suggested that people with signs of early memory decline who ate grapes twice a day saw improved attention span and working memory. The scientists proposed that a regular intake of grapes may provide a protective effect against early decline associated with Alzheimer's disease.

Serves 4

2 large cooked skinless, boneless chicken breast fillets, cubed

4 handfuls of seedless grapes, halved

4 celery sticks, thinly sliced (optional)

1 red onion, diced

1 fresh red chilli, deseeded and finely chopped

A handful of fresh basil leaves, torn

1 tbsp toasted flaked almonds

1 tbsp natural yogurt

1 dessertspoon extra-light mayonnaise

4 wholemeal pitta breads

A handful of rocket (optional)

In a large bowl, combine the chicken, grapes, celery, onion, chilli, basil, almonds, yogurt and mayonnaise. Mix well, then cover and chill in the fridge until you're ready to serve.

Stuff the pitta pockets with the chicken salad and a handful of rocket if you like.

Smoked chicken, mango and avocado salad

Avocados are delicious with the sweet mango in this recipe. They contain vitamins C, E, K and B6 as well as riboflavin, niacin, folate, pantothenic acid and potassium. They also provide a little lutein, beta-carotene and omega-3 fatty acids, which makes them a super brain food. Although most of the calories in an avocado come from fat, it's the right kind of fat to eat, so enjoy up to half an avocado as an average serving. They will help to keep you full and satisfied.

Serves 2

1 avocado, halved and stoned

2 tsp lemon juice

1 small mango

3 dessertspoons extra virgin olive oil

2 tsp cider vinegar

1 tsp wholegrain mustard

1 tsp clear honey

Salt and freshly ground black pepper

A handful of watercress

50g cooked beetroot, thinly sliced

200g smoked chicken, thinly sliced

Scoop the avocado flesh out of its skin, then slice or dice and place in a shallow bowl with the lemon juice.

Peel the mango, then cut it in half on either side of the central pit and slice or dice the flesh.

Whisk the olive oil with the vinegar, mustard, honey and some salt and pepper. Remove the avocado from the lemon juice and mix the juice into the dressing.

Arrange the watercress and beetroot on two plates or in a salad bowl, then add the avocado and mango. Drizzle the vinaigrette over the salad and top with the slices of smoked chicken. Serve immediately.

Rocket pesto to liven up your sandwiches and toppings

Although all nuts have health benefits, walnuts are a head above the rest. They are the best nut source of alpha-linolenic acid (ALA), the plant form of the essential and anti-inflammatory omega-3 fats. They also contain a unique polyphenol, pedunculagin, which is thought to help reduce brain inflammation. A handful of mixed nuts three to four times a week makes a nourishing snack. Alternatively, use walnuts in pestos, like this one, or scatter them over salads. I use this rocket pesto as a pizza sauce or to spread on top of white fish fillets or chicken breast fillets.

Serves 4

4 handfuls of rocket

2 handfuls of fresh basil

2 large garlic cloves, crushed

4 tbsp chopped walnuts

4 tbsp extra virgin olive oil (add more if necessary)

A pinch of salt

Put all the ingredients in a blender and pulse until ground into a paste. You may need to add a little more oil to get it to come together. Cover and refrigerate for up to four days or double the batch and freeze for later.

Spinach and basil pesto

This bright green pesto is full of flavour. Although there's no magic pill to prevent cognitive decline, no one single brain food can promise us a miracle either. A healthy dietary pattern, including lots of vegetables, legumes, fruits, seafood, healthy oil and whole grains, is key. That said, emerging research shows that the best brain foods are the same ones that protect our hearts and blood vessels too. Leafy green vegetables such as spinach contain brain-healthy nutrients like vitamin K, lutein, folate and beta-carotene. Research suggests that these plant-based foods may help to slow cognitive decline.

Serves 4

100g Parmesan cheese, grated

4 handfuls of baby spinach

4 handfuls of fresh basil leaves

2 garlic cloves, crushed

4 tbsp extra virgin olive oil

2 tbsp lemon juice

Salt and freshly ground black pepper

Put all the ingredients in a food processor or blender. Turn on the machine and blend for 30 seconds. Stop and scrape down the sides with a spatula and blend again until smooth. Taste and add more salt and pepper if necessary. If you like a thinner pesto, add a little more olive oil.

Cover and refrigerate for up to four days or double the batch and freeze for later. This is a great accompaniment to veggies dishes, chicken and fish or you can enjoy it as a spread on high-fibre crackers or sourdough bread.

Pesto pulses

This quick and easy salad has only four ingredients and takes less than 60 seconds to assemble! Tinned chickpeas are the key shortcut to prepping this versatile and healthy Mediterranean dish, and taking shortcuts is well worth it for the health benefits when you're time poor. The soluble fibre in chickpeas can help to lower LDL cholesterol (the 'bad' cholesterol) in the blood. Chickpeas also contain choline, which aids in the transmission of nerve impulses and helps to reduce inflammation. Choline is also important for learning and memory.

Serves 4

1 x 400g tin of chickpeas, drained and rinsed

150g fresh mozzarella, chopped

8 plum tomatoes, quartered

3 tbsp pesto (page 105 or 106)

Salt and freshly ground black pepper

A large handful of fresh basil, chopped (optional)

In a medium bowl, combine the chickpeas, mozzarella, tomatoes and pesto. Gently stir to combine, then season with salt and pepper to taste. Garnish with fresh basil if desired and serve.

Herby quinoa

Quinoa replaces the bulgur wheat traditionally used in this Mediterranean dish. This naturally gluten-free recipe provides a complete plant protein with all nine essential amino acids. Citrus fruits such as lemons are excellent sources of vitamin C and flavonoids, which may help to lower our risk of stroke as part of a diverse and healthy overall eating pattern, according to the American Heart Association.

Serves 4

180g uncooked red, white or black quinoa (or a mixture)

500ml water or low-sodium vegetable broth (gluten free if necessary)

1 head of broccoli, broken into small florets

Zest and juice of 1 lemon

3 tbsp extra virgin olive oil

16 plum tomatoes, diced

1 red onion, finely chopped

2 large handfuls of fresh parsley, chopped

2 handfuls of fresh basil, chopped

A handful of fresh mint, chopped

Pinch of chilli flakes

Salt and freshly ground black pepper

Sunflower seeds or pine nuts, to garnish (optional)

Rinse the quinoa, then put in a saucepan with the water or broth. Bring to the boil, then reduce the heat to a simmer, cover the pan and cook for 15 minutes, until all the water has been absorbed and the quinoa is tender. Fluff up the quinoa with a fork and set aside to cool.

Meanwhile, blanch the broccoli in boiling water for 2 minutes. Remove from the water with a slotted spoon and place in an ice bath to stop it from cooking further. Drain thoroughly.

In a large bowl, whisk together the lemon zest and juice and olive oil. Stir in the quinoa, broccoli, tomatoes, red onion, parsley, basil, mint and a pinch of chilli flakes. Season to taste with salt and pepper.

Top with sunflower seeds or pine nuts (if using). Serve at room temperature or chilled.

Jazzed-up quinoa leftovers

If I have leftover quinoa in the fridge, I sometimes add in fresh basil, chopped red pepper and tomato and diced red onion. Quinoa contains all nine essential amino acids and is a great way to get your fibre. It's a source of iron, which keeps our oxygen-carrying red blood cells healthy, thereby supporting brain health. It also contains vitamin B2, which keeps brain and muscle cells healthy.

Serves 4

1 tbsp extra virgin olive oil

2 garlic cloves, crushed

2 large eggs

8 handfuls of baby spinach, roughly chopped

2 tbsp grated mozzarella or Parmesan cheese, plus extra to serve

Leftover cooked quinoa

Salt and freshly ground black pepper

A pinch of chilli flakes (optional)

Heat the oil in a small frying pan, then add the garlic and cook for 30 seconds.

Whisk the eggs in a small bowl, then pour into the pan. Once the eggs start to cook, add the spinach, cheese and cooked quinoa and mix together. Season with salt and pepper or some chilli flakes.

Transfer to a serving bowl and scatter over a little more cheese.

Baked stuffed peppers

This tasty, immune-boosting, vitamin C-rich pepper and parsley lunch contains buckets of other nutrients too. The spinach, capers, chilli and pine nuts contribute plenty of antioxidant-rich phytonutrients, accompanied by the traditional Mediterranean monounsaturated olive oil. Olive oil contains a significant amount of fat-soluble vitamins E and K, both of which are important for memory and cognitive function.

Serves 2

2 peppers, halved and deseeded

2 tbsp olive oil, plus 1 tsp for drizzling

Freshly ground black pepper

1 slice of wholegrain sourdough bread

1 fresh red or green chilli, deseeded and finely chopped

2 tbsp pine nuts

2 tbsp grated Parmesan cheese

2 tsp capers

A large handful of fresh parsley, roughly chopped

4 large handfuls of baby spinach

Preheat the oven to 180°C.

Put the peppers in a roasting tin, cut sides up, then drizzle with the teaspoon of oil and a little black pepper. Bake in the oven for 20 minutes.

Meanwhile, toast the bread, then blitz into rough crumbs in a food processor or finely crumble with your hands. Mix with the chilli, pine nuts, Parmesan, capers, parsley and the remaining 2 tablespoons of oil.

Boil the kettle. Put the spinach in a colander, then pour over the boiling water to wilt the leaves. Press out as much water as possible.

Divide the spinach between the peppers, then top with the breadcrumb mixture. Return to the oven for 15 minutes, then remove and serve.

Chicken with cannellini beans

Beans contain several great nutrients, including folate, which is important for a healthy nervous system. Dried beans contain nearly double the folate that tinned beans do, so it's worth cooking them from their dried form. However, tinned beans still contain more folate than many foods and are very convenient when you need to put together a quick lunch in minutes.

Serves 4

4 large grilled chicken breast fillets

4 tbsp extra virgin olive oil

3 tbsp lemon juice

Freshly ground black pepper

2 x 400g tins of cannellini beans, drained and rinsed

300g cherry tomatoes, halved

4 spring onions, thinly sliced

2 tbsp chopped fresh mint

Crusty wholemeal bread, to serve

Slice each grilled chicken fillet into strips on the diagonal.

Whisk together the olive oil and lemon juice in a small jug. Season to taste with freshly ground black pepper.

Put the beans, tomatoes, spring onions and mint in a serving bowl, then toss with the dressing.

Serve the salad on plates with a sliced chicken fillet on top and some crusty wholemeal bread on the side.

Lamb meatballs

Studies that have compared the TMD and the traditional Japanese diet to our typical Western diet have shown that the risk of depression is up to 35% lower in those who eat a traditional diet. Researchers account for this difference because these traditional diets tend to be higher in vegetables, fruits, unprocessed grains and fish and seafood and contain only modest amounts of lean meat and dairy. Although meat is eaten sparingly as part of the TMD, this unique Greek-style lamb dish is worth including.

Serves 4

400g lamb mince

4 garlic cloves, crushed

3 tbsp chopped fresh parsley

1 tbsp dried oregano

1 tbsp ground cinnamon

1 tsp dried basil

Preheat the oven to 180°C.

Mix all the ingredients together in a large bowl until well combined. Form into small meatballs and arrange in a baking dish. Bake in the oven for 20 minutes.

Serve with a simple tomato sauce (page 113), roasted vegetables, wild rice or quinoa.

Simple tomato sauce

I love this lycopene-rich sauce because it holds in the fridge for up to five days, but you can freeze it too. It's great with roast vegetables, chicken and fish or as a base for a soup, not to mention as a sauce for pasta or homemade pizza (see page 139).

Serves 4

1 tbsp olive oil

1 onion, sliced

2 garlic cloves, minced

2 x 400g tins of chopped or whole plum tomatoes

Salt and freshly ground black pepper

Heat the oil in a saucepan over a medium heat. Add the onions and cook until soft. Add the garlic and cook for 1 minute more.

Add the tomatoes and reduce to your desired consistency (cook for longer for a thicker consistency). Season to taste with salt and pepper.

LUNCH

Sore throat remedy

For those times when you need a pick-me-up, this sore throat remedy tastes so much better than the commercial ones. Don't give this to young children, as it's too spicy for them, plus children under one year of age should not have honey.

Serves 1

60ml just-boiled water

½ tsp local honey

60ml cold water
(to make the drink
lukewarm)

1 tbsp raw apple cider
vinegar

Pinch of cayenne pepper

Pinch of freshly grated
or ground ginger or ½
clove of crushed garlic
(optional)

Pour the just-boiled water in a mug, then add the honey and stir until it dissolves. Add the remaining ingredients and stir together, then drink it like a shot.

Dinner

VEGGIE SIDES & MAINS

Feta, toasted hazelnut and courgette strips

Feta is traditionally produced using sheep's milk (or a blend of sheep's and goat's milk). Most producers use pasteurised milk, which means the feta is not as salty and tangy as the original cheese. If you want to liven up the flavour, sprinkle it with some aromatic herbs like oregano or add some chopped olives as a garnish.

Hazelnuts and other tree nuts have an impressive store of monounsaturated fat, vitamin E and minerals such as copper and magnesium, all of which help to manage blood pressure levels and inflammation.

Serves 4

2 tbsp olive oil

3 large courgettes, thickly sliced lengthways

Zest of 1 lemon

120g feta cheese, crumbled

4 dessertspoons toasted hazelnuts

1 fresh red chilli, deseeded and chopped

A handful of fresh mint leaves, torn

Salt and freshly ground black pepper

Lightly brush a cast iron griddle pan with a little of the olive oil and set it on a high heat. Add the courgette strips to the hot pan and grill for 2 minutes on each side, until lightly charred.

Divide the grilled courgettes between four plates, then scatter over some lemon zest. Top with the crumbled feta, toasted hazelnuts, fresh chilli and mint. Drizzle over the rest of the oil and some seasoning. Serve warm or at room temperature.

Mozzarella and fig salad

I adore ripe fresh figs on a cheeseboard or in a Mediterranean salad.
Figs are high in natural sugars, minerals and soluble fibre. Figs are also a
good source of minerals, including potassium, calcium, magnesium, iron
and copper. They also contain small amounts of antioxidant vitamins A,
E and K, which contribute to health and wellness.

Serves 4

200g fine green beans,
trimmed

6 ripe figs, quartered

1 spring onion, thinly
sliced

1 x 150g ball mozzarella,
drained and chopped or
torn into chunks

50g hazelnuts, toasted
and roughly chopped

A handful of fresh basil
leaves, torn

3 tbsp extra virgin olive
oil

3 tbsp balsamic vinegar

1 tbsp fig relish

Salt and freshly ground
black pepper

Blanch the beans in a large pot of boiling water for 5
minutes. Drain and rinse under cold water to stop them
from cooking.

Cut the beans in half and pat dry with kitchen paper.
Arrange in a serving bowl with the figs, spring onion,
mozzarella, hazelnuts and basil around and on top.

Put the oil, vinegar, fig relish and some salt and pepper
in a jar with a screw-top lid. Shake to combine, then
pour over the salad just before serving.

DINNER

Pomegranate jewel salad with feta

I love the colour and textures in this Mediterranean salad. Just looking at it lifts my mood. Pomegranate seeds aren't just a wonderful contrast to the creamy whiteness of the feta – they are high in vitamin C, potassium and fibre too.

Serves 4

2 red peppers

2 aubergines, cut into chunks

4 tbsp extra virgin olive oil

1 tsp ground cinnamon

Salt and freshly ground black pepper

200g mangetout

1 red onion, thinly sliced

200g feta cheese, crumbled

Seeds of 1 pomegranate

A handful of fresh basil leaves, torn

For the dressing:

1 small garlic clove, crushed

5 tbsp extra virgin olive oil

2 tbsp pomegranate molasses

1 tbsp lemon juice

Preheat the oven to 180°C. Heat the grill to its highest setting.

Cut the peppers into quarters and place on a baking sheet, skin side up. Grill until blackened, then put in a ziplock bag, seal and leave for 5 minutes. When the peppers are cool enough to handle, peel off the skins and discard, then set the peppers aside.

Meanwhile, put the aubergines on a baking tray. Drizzle with the olive oil and cinnamon and season well. Roast in the oven for 30 minutes, until golden and softened.

Combine all the dressing ingredients and mix well.

To serve, put the peppers, aubergines, mangetout and onion on a large serving plate. Scatter over the feta and pomegranate seeds. Pour the dressing over, then finish with the basil leaves.

Artichoke and bean salad

Pulses or beans are colourful, versatile and highly nutritious. Use these prebiotic babies in soups, stews and salads where possible. Your gut microbiome will thank you.

Serves 4

1 x 175g jar of artichoke hearts in oil

1 tbsp sun-dried tomato paste

1 tsp white wine vinegar

Salt and freshly ground black pepper

1 x 400g tin of cannellini beans, drained and rinsed

12 vine-ripened tomatoes, quartered

A handful of pitted black Kalamata olives

4 spring onions, thinly sliced

200g soft goat's cheese, crumbled

A few toasted walnuts, chopped

Drain the jar of artichokes, reserving 3 tablespoons of the oil. Pour the oil into a bowl and stir in the sun-dried tomato paste and vinegar until smooth. Season to taste.

Roughly chop the artichokes and tip into a large bowl with the cannellini beans, tomatoes, olives, spring onions and half the goat's cheese. Stir in the artichoke oil dressing, then transfer to a serving bowl and season to taste.

Crumble over the remaining goat's cheese and walnuts, then serve.

DINNER

Tomato and mint salad

Simple but perfect. Instead of mint leaves, try basil and tomato as a side dish with dinner. Some people prefer a drizzle of balsamic to lemon zest. Mint is a calming and soothing herb that has been used for thousands of years to help soothe upset stomachs. It is thought to increase bile secretion and encourage bile flow, which helps digestion. It's one of the easiest herbs to grow – in fact, you might need to contain it in a pot so that it doesn't smother other, more delicate garden herbs.

Serves 4

400g cherry tomatoes, halved

1 small red onion, finely chopped

2 handfuls of fresh mint leaves, torn

Extra virgin olive oil, for drizzling

Salt and freshly ground black pepper

Zest of 1 lemon

Spread out the halved tomatoes on a serving plate. Sprinkle the onion and mint over the tomatoes. This can be kept covered at room temperature at this stage, ahead of serving.

Just before serving, drizzle with extra virgin olive oil, season with salt and pepper and finely grate the lemon zest on top.

Honey-roasted vegetables

Roasted vegetables are easy peasy to prepare and save time with
minimal washing up required. You can use all the extra veggies you have
lying around and the delicious caramelised tray bake will give you a
filling, low-calorie, high-fibre accompaniment that can be enjoyed on its
own or mixed with a tin of chickpeas, some roast chicken or fish.

Serves 3

1 red pepper

1 red onion, peeled

1 courgette

1 sweet potato, peeled

1 garlic clove, crushed

1 tbsp olive oil

2 tsp honey

Preheat the oven to 180°C.

Chop the red pepper, onion, courgette and sweet potato
into similar bite-sized pieces and place in a bowl.

In a small cup, mix the garlic, olive oil and honey
together. Pour over the vegetables and toss to coat.

Spread the vegetables out on a baking tray and roast in
the oven for 30–40 minutes. Serve warm.

Roast Mediterranean vegetable, chickpea and quinoa salad

Researchers have found that rosemary may be good for the brain. Rosemary contains carnosic acid, which helps to protect against free radical damage. In some studies, even just the smell of rosemary has been shown to improve concentration and, to a lesser extent, mood.

This is delicious with some crumbled feta cheese dotted on top too. I make a double batch, as it keeps well in the fridge to accompany some white fish or chicken later in the week or just pop the extra batch into the freezer.

Serves 4

2 peppers (any colour)

2 courgettes

1 red onion

1 aubergine

1 x 400g tin of chickpeas, drained and rinsed

12 pitted black Kalamata olives

2 tbsp olive oil

2 tsp dried herbs de Provence

1 tsp dried thyme

Salt and freshly ground black pepper

A few fresh rosemary sprigs

150g quinoa

300ml water

1 tsp bouillon powder

For the dressing:

Zest and juice of 1 small lemon

4 tbsp extra virgin olive oil

1 tsp honey

1 tsp Dijon mustard

Preheat the oven to 180°C.

Chop all the vegetables into similar bite-sized pieces and place in a large bowl with the chickpeas and olives.

Sprinkle over the olive oil, herbes de Provence and thyme and season with a little salt and pepper. Mix well, then spread onto two small baking trays in a single layer so that they can roast well. Nestle the rosemary sprigs into the mixture on each tray.

Roast in the oven for 20–30 minutes, until the vegetables are just soft. Set aside to cool and remove the sprigs of rosemary.

Meanwhile, rinse the quinoa in a sieve under a running tap for a few seconds. Drain and put in a pot with the water and bouillon powder. Bring to the boil, then turn down the heat, cover the pot and simmer for 15 minutes. The water should have all been absorbed, but if not, drain it off. Transfer from the pot to a large bowl and fluff up with a fork to cool.

Put all the dressing ingredients into a small bowl and whisk to combine.

Add the roast vegetables and chickpeas to the quinoa and pour over the dressing. Toss to combine and serve.

Halloumi and garlic-dressed vegetables with quinoa

These high-fibre veggies are delicious with any cheese, but grilled halloumi is a great semi-hard brined cheese made from a mixture of goat's and sheep's milk (or occasionally cow's milk) that originally came from Cyprus.

Serves 4

4 beetroot, peeled and cut into chunks

4 medium sweet potatoes, scrubbed and cut into similar-sized chunks as the beetroots

4 red onions, thickly sliced into wedges

2 tbsp olive oil

Salt and freshly ground black pepper

200g quinoa

1 litre vegetable stock

2 x 250g packs of halloumi, each block cut into 6 slices

Chopped fresh parsley, to garnish

For the dressing:

1 garlic bulb

3 tbsp extra virgin olive oil

1 tbsp lemon juice

1 tsp clear honey

Preheat the oven to 180°C.

Put the beetroot, sweet potatoes and red onions on a large roasting tray.

Cut the top off the garlic bulb and drizzle with a little of the olive oil, then pop it onto the roasting tray too. You'll be using this later for the dressing.

Season the vegetables and pour the remaining oil over them. Roast in the oven for about 40 minutes, turning the vegetables halfway through.

Meanwhile, put the quinoa and stock in a pot over a high heat. Bring to the boil, then reduce the heat, cover the pot with a lid and simmer for 15 minutes. Drain the quinoa and return to the pot, off the heat, and fluff up with a fork.

When the vegetables are done, set the garlic bulb aside and stir the roasted veg through the quinoa.

Put a cast iron griddle pan over a high heat. Add the halloumi slices and grill for 1 minute on each side.

To make the dressing, squeeze the roasted garlic from the bulb into a small bowl. Add the extra virgin olive oil, lemon juice and honey and whisk to combine.

To serve, divide the veggie quinoa between plates. Top with the grilled halloumi, then pour over the dressing. Garnish with a little chopped fresh parsley.

Vegetable and feta filo tartlet

Light and tasty, this quick veggie supper looks super colourful too.
Boost the protein and fibre levels by serving the tartlet with a mixed
bean salad.

Serves 4

2 tbsp olive oil

2 red onions, cut into
chunky wedges

2 courgettes, sliced

1 aubergine, sliced

3 sheets of filo pastry

Salt and freshly ground
black pepper

12 cherry tomatoes,
halved

A few artichoke hearts,
chopped

Drizzle of balsamic
vinegar

120g feta cheese,
crumbled

2 tsp dried oregano

Mixed bean salad (page
89), to serve

Lightly dressed mixed
salad leaves, to serve

Preheat the oven to 180°C. Put a baking tray in the oven
to heat up.

Rub a little of the oil onto your hands, then massage the
sliced onions, courgettes and aubergine. Pop them onto
a hot cast iron griddle pan to char them, then set aside.

Remove the baking tray from the oven and brush with
a little oil. Brush a sheet of filo pastry with oil, then top
with another sheet, brush with a little more oil and
repeat with the final sheet. Transfer the pastry to the
hot tray, pushing it into the edges a little.

Arrange the charred veg on top and season well. Pop on
the cherry tomatoes and artichokes, then drizzle with
the balsamic vinegar and any remaining oil. Crumble
on the feta and sprinkle with the oregano.

Bake in the oven for about 20 minutes, until crisp and
golden. Serve with a mixed bean salad and some lightly
dressed mixed salad leaves.

Puy lentil shepherd's pie

Legumes, including lentils, are a source of all three forms of dietary fibre: soluble fibre, insoluble fibre and resistant starch. These different fibres offer many protective effects. A healthy fibre intake of over 25g per day can help to lower inflammation, improve weight control, lower the risk of digestive disorders and enhance immune function.

Serves 4

1 tbsp olive oil

3 carrots, diced

2 celery sticks, finely chopped

1 onion, finely chopped

1 garlic clove, crushed

1 x 400g tin of chopped tomatoes

200g Puy lentils

500ml vegetable stock

1 bay leaf

1 tbsp tomato purée

1 tsp paprika

Fresh thyme leaves, to garnish

For the mash topping:

800g sweet potatoes, peeled and cut into large chunks

A handful of fresh chives, chopped

2 tbsp freshly grated Parmesan cheese

Pinch of freshly grated nutmeg

Salt and freshly ground black pepper

To serve:

leafy green salad

crusty bread

Heat the oil in a saucepan over a medium heat. Add the carrots, celery, onion and garlic and cook gently until they soften.

Stir in the tomatoes, lentils, stock, bay leaf, tomato purée and paprika and simmer gently for about 25 minutes. You may need to add more stock or water, as lentils suck up a lot of liquid. Don't add any salt until after the lentils are cooked, otherwise it toughens them.

Meanwhile, put the sweet potatoes in a pot and cover with cold salted water. Bring to the boil, then reduce the heat and simmer until soft. Drain the sweet potatoes and mash with the chives, Parmesan, nutmeg and some salt and pepper.

When the lentils are done, season with salt and pepper and spoon into a baking dish. Spoon the mash over and use the back of a spoon to smooth the top.

Bake in the oven for 20 minutes. Garnish with fresh thyme leaves and serve with a leafy green salad and crusty bread.

Mushroom Bourguignon

Mushrooms are high in the mineral selenium, which has been found to prevent inflammation and improve the immune response to infection by stimulating the production of killer T-cells. Mushrooms' beta-glucan fibres also stimulate the immune system to fight cancer cells.

Serves 4

4 tbsp olive oil

10 shallots, peeled

6 carrots, roughly chopped

2 celery sticks, finely chopped

3 garlic cloves, peeled

4–5 very large Portobello mushrooms, stalks removed and discarded and cut into bite-sized chunks

Salt and freshly ground black pepper

1 bottle of red wine

300ml vegetable stock

6 sprigs of fresh thyme

3 bay leaves

2 courgettes, roughly chopped

300g mixed mushrooms, quartered

Grilled sourdough bread or mashed sweet potatoes, to serve

Place a large pot over a low heat. Add 2 tablespoons of the olive oil, then add the shallots and fry for about 15 minutes, until lightly golden. Add the carrots, celery and garlic and increase the heat to medium. Cook until the carrots are golden and soft. Remove the veg from the pot and set aside.

Season the Portobello mushrooms with salt and pepper. Add the remaining 2 tablespoons of oil to the pot and increase the heat to medium-high. Add the Portobello mushrooms and cook until browned.

Reduce the heat to medium, then add the wine, vegetable stock, thyme and bay leaves and bring up to a simmer. Reduce the heat to low, cover the pot and simmer for 45 minutes, stirring occasionally.

Add the cooked vegetables to the pot along with the courgette and mixed mushrooms. Cover the pot again and simmer for 30 minutes more.

Serve with grilled sourdough bread or mashed sweet potatoes.

Chilli non carne

Garlic was widely used in the TMD and as a medicine throughout ancient history. It belongs to the genus *Allium* and is closely related to onions, leeks, chives, spring onions and shallots. Garlic is best prepared and chopped about 15 minutes before you intend to use it to get the benefits of the antimicrobial and antioxidant properties from the allicin it contains.

Serves 4

Splash of olive oil

1 large onion, chopped finely

2 garlic cloves, crushed

2 carrots, diced

1 red pepper, deseeded and diced

1 green pepper, deseeded and diced

1 tsp chilli flakes

1 tsp ground cumin

2 x 400g tins of chopped tomatoes

1 x 400g tin of red kidney beans, drained and rinsed

1 x 400g tin of lentils, drained and rinsed

100g green beans, chopped

1 tbsp tomato puree

250ml water

To serve:

Brown and wild rice

Diced avocado

Greek or natural yogurt

Fresh coriander leaves

Pitta bread

Lime wedges

Heat a splash of olive oil in a wide saucepan over a medium heat. Add the onion and cook for 3 minutes, stirring often, then add the garlic and cook for 1 minute.

Add the carrots and peppers and stir fry for 3–4 minutes. Add the chilli and cumin and cook for 2 minutes.

Add the chopped tomatoes, kidney beans, lentils, green beans, tomato purée and a cup of water. Simmer for 25 minutes, until the chilli has thickened.

Ladle on top of a bed of brown and wild rice. Top with diced avocado, a generous spoonful of yogurt and fresh coriander leaves. Serve with pitta bread and lime wedges on the side.

Garlic, tomato and mozzarella pizza

Shop-bought pizza never tastes as good as homemade. You can simply add as many leftover roasted veg and odds and ends from the fridge as possible to vary your homemade creations.

   Balsamic vinegar is a traditional Mediterranean ingredient in salad dressings, marinades and many other foods. It has a distinctive flavour that is often described as bold, tart and complex. Acetic acid is the active compound in balsamic vinegar. It contains strains of probiotics that help digestion and promote good gut and immune health.

Makes 1 pizza

2 spring onions, chopped

2 tbsp white balsamic vinegar

Salt and freshly ground black pepper

1 batch of pizza dough (page 139)

1 tbsp extra virgin olive oil, plus extra for drizzling

1 garlic clove, very thinly sliced

A handful of vine-ripened tomatoes, thinly sliced

1 medium ball of fresh mozzarella, drained and torn

5 pitted black olives, sliced

5 fresh basil leaves

1 handful of rocket

Pinch of chilli flakes

Preheat the oven to 180°C. Lightly oil a pizza pan.

Place the spring onions in 1 tablespoon of the vinegar along with a pinch of salt to lightly pickle while you bake the pizza bases.

Roll out the dough into a large circle that will fit your pizza pan. Bake in the oven for 10–15 minutes, until the dough is cooked and golden.

Drizzle the cooked side of the pizza base with the tablespoon of oil. Season with salt and pepper, scatter over the sliced garlic and return to the oven for about 5 minutes more, until the garlic is golden and the dough is crisp.

Remove the pizza from the oven and top with the tomatoes, mozzarella, olives, some of the basil, the remaining tablespoon of vinegar and a drizzle of oil. Drain the spring onions and sprinkle them over along with the rocket and remaining basil leaves. Season everything with lots of black pepper and some chilli flakes. Cut into slices to serve.

Rocket and goat's cheese pizza

Homemade pizza can be a delicious indulgence now and then. You can enhance its nutritional value by keeping the crust thin, using a low-salt and low-fat cheese, and topping it with greens just before you serve it. Cheese contributes both protein and minerals such as calcium and phosphorous, and the tomato sauce is a good source of the antioxidant lycopene.

Makes 1 pizza

For the dough:

180ml warm water

½ sachet of dried yeast (10g)

250g strong white flour

Pinch of salt

1 tbsp olive oil

For the topping:

Olive oil, for brushing (optional)

Simple tomato sauce (page 113)

150g soft goat's cheese

A handful of rocket

To make the dough, add the yeast to the warm water. Set aside for 10 minutes to allow the yeast to activate.

Sieve the flour into a bowl and stir in the salt. Make a well in the centre. Pour the yeast mix and the oil into the well and stir to bring the mix together into a dough. Turn out onto a floured work surface and knead for 10 minutes, until smooth and elastic. Alternatively, you can use a stand mixer fitted with a dough hook for this.

Put the dough into a large lightly oiled bowl. Cover with cling film and leave in a warm, draught-free place for 1½–2 hours, until it has doubled in size.

Preheat the oven to 220°C. Lightly oil a pizza pan.

Roll out the dough into a large circle that will fit your pizza pan.

Brush the edges of the dough with a little olive oil to make it crispier if that's the way you like it. Spread the base with the tomato sauce, then bake in the oven for 10–15 minutes, until the dough is cooked and golden.

Dot over the goat's cheese after it comes out of the oven – it will gently melt from the residual heat – and top with a handful of rocket. Cut into slices to serve.

Veggie medley

Get five vegetables and two legumes in one meal with this vibrant, fibre-rich prebiotic mix. I like the leftovers the following day with some grilled chicken.

Serves 4

1 tbsp olive oil

2 leeks, thinly sliced

1 red onion, thinly sliced

3 garlic cloves, finely chopped

2 tsp ground coriander

2 tsp ground cumin

1 tsp chilli flakes

¼ tsp ground cinnamon

Salt and freshly ground black pepper

1 x 400g tin of chopped tomatoes

1 x 400g tin of chickpeas, drained and rinsed

100g dried red lentils

2 large sweet potatoes, unpeeled and cut into small chunks

1 red pepper, deseeded and cut into strips

1 yellow pepper, deseeded and cut into strips

Zest and juice of 1 large orange

400ml water

A large handful of fresh coriander, roughly chopped, to serve

40g mixed nuts (hazelnuts, pecans, almond and walnuts), toasted and roughly chopped

Natural or Greek yogurt, to serve

Heat the oil in a big pot over a medium heat. Add the leeks and onion and sauté for 15 minutes, until well softened. Add the garlic and cook for another couple of minutes.

Stir in the ground coriander, cumin, chilli flakes and cinnamon. Cook for 2 minutes, stirring occasionally. Season with salt and plenty of freshly ground black pepper.

Add the chopped tomatoes, chickpeas, lentils, sweet potatoes, peppers, orange zest and juice and water and bring up to a simmer. Cook for 15 minutes, adding a splash of water if it looks too dry and stirring occasionally, until the potatoes are tender but not breaking apart.

Remove the pot from the heat and ladle the stew into bowls. Top with fresh coriander, mixed nuts and some natural or Greek yogurt.

Aubergine, chickpea and lemon bulgur

Varying your carbohydrates can be fun sometimes. Bulgur is a partially cooked and cracked whole wheat grain that is common in the Middle East and Mediterranean basin. It has a nice nutty flavour.

Serves 4

2 aubergines, sliced lengthways into long strips

5 tbsp olive oil

Salt and freshly ground black pepper

250g bulgur wheat

1 litre water

2 large red onions, thinly sliced

1 tbsp ground cumin

1 x 400g tin of chickpeas, drained and rinsed

Freshly grated Parmesan, to serve

For the dressing:

3 tbsp extra virgin olive oil

2 garlic cloves, crushed

Zest and juice of 1 large lemon

A large handful of fresh coriander, chopped

A large handful of fresh mint, chopped

Preheat the oven to 180°C.

Divide the aubergine ribbons between two baking sheets. Brush with 4 tablespoons of the olive oil and season with a little salt and pepper, then roast in the oven for 15 minutes.

Meanwhile, put the bulgur in a pot with the water. Bring to the boil, then reduce the heat and simmer for 15 minutes, until soft.

Heat the remaining one tablespoon of oil in a pan over a medium heat. Add the onions and sauté until golden and soft, then add the cumin and cook for 1 minute more, stirring all the time.

Drain the bulgur and mix it in with the onions. Add the chickpeas and season to taste with salt and pepper.

To make the dressing, put all the ingredients in a small bowl or jar with some seasoning and whisk to combine.

To serve, spoon some bulgur onto each plate. Top with the roasted aubergines, a drizzle of dressing and some freshly grated Parmesan cheese.

Gigantes plaki

Gigantes plaki is Greek for 'giant baked beans'. Butter beans are an economical source of plant protein and are naturally low in fat, despite their name. Beans and legumes in general are a good source of B vitamins (especially folate), iron, zinc, calcium and magnesium. They are also an abundant source of fibre (both insoluble and soluble) plus resistant starch for colonic health benefits.

Serves 4

400g dried butter beans

3 tbsp olive oil

1 red onion, finely chopped

2 garlic cloves, finely chopped

2 heaped tbsp tomato purée

800g very sweet, ripe tomatoes, roughly chopped

1 red pepper, deseeded and finely chopped

2 tsp dried oregano

Salt and freshly ground black pepper

3 tbsp chopped flat-leaf parsley

Omelette or poached eggs, to serve (optional)

Put the butter beans in a large glass bowl and cover with plenty of cold water. Cover the bowl and allow to soak overnight.

Drain and rinse the butter beans, then pop them into a pot and cover with fresh cold water. Bring to the boil, then reduce the heat and simmer for about 50 minutes, until slightly tender. Don't let them get mushy. Drain and set aside.

Preheat the oven to 180°C.

Heat the olive oil in a casserole over a medium heat. Add the onion and garlic and cook for 10 minutes, until softened. Add the tomato purée and cook for 1 minute more. Add the tomatoes, red pepper and oregano and simmer for 2 minutes. Season generously, then stir in the beans.

Transfer the pan to the oven and bake, uncovered, for about 30 minutes. Remove from the oven and allow to cool slightly.

To serve, drizzle with a little more olive oil and scatter the chopped fresh parsley on top. Serve with an omelette or poached eggs for extra protein if you like.

FISH

White fish and fennel gratin

Individual ramekin dishes are very handy when entertaining – I always put extra on for hungry visitors. You can use any white fish you like or a combination of a few different types of white fish in this dish. It's a good idea to have a minimum of two designated fish dinners per week: one white and one oily. White fish is generally low in fat, making it one of the healthiest alternatives to red or processed meat. White fish is also a source of omega-3 fatty acids, but at much lower levels than oily fish. Some white fish, such as sea bream, sea bass, turbot and halibut, may contain similar levels of certain pollutants as oily fish, so consult with a dietitian if you are pregnant or planning a pregnancy. Also, try to choose seafood that has been caught or produced in a way that allows stocks to replenish and that won't cause unnecessary damage to marine animals and plants.

Serves 6

3 tbsp olive oil

1 large onion, thinly sliced

1 fennel bulb, trimmed and thinly sliced

3 large garlic cloves, thinly sliced

1 heaped tsp coriander seeds, lightly crushed

150ml white wine

2 x 400g tins of chopped tomatoes with herbs

2 tbsp tomato purée

Good pinch of saffron

1 bay leaf

Salt and freshly ground black pepper

1 tbsp freshly squeezed lemon juice

1 small bunch of fresh flat-leaf parsley, roughly chopped

6 large white fish fillets (such as cod, hake, haddock or pollock), skinned, deboned and cut into chunks

350g raw peeled prawns

100g sourdough breadcrumbs

60g Parmesan cheese, finely grated

green salad, to serve

Preheat the oven to 180°C.

Heat the oil in a large, wide non-stick frying pan. Add the onion, fennel, garlic and coriander seeds and gently sauté for 15 minutes, stirring regularly, until the vegetables are softened and lightly coloured.

Pour the wine into the pan, then add the tomatoes, tomato purée, saffron and bay leaf. Season to taste and bring to a gentle simmer. Cook for about 15 minutes, stirring occasionally, until the tomatoes have reduced.

Stir the lemon juice and most of the parsley into the pan, then pop the raw fish pieces and prawns on top and stir well. Cover tightly with a lid and simmer gently over a medium heat for 4–5 minutes, until the fish is almost cooked. Gently stir a couple of times as the fish cooks, taking care not to break it up.

Ladle the hot tomato and fish mixture into six ramekin dishes.

Mix the sourdough breadcrumbs, cheese, remaining parsley and a little ground black pepper together, then sprinkle over the top of the fish.

Place the ramekins on a baking tray and bake in the oven for 20 minutes, until the topping is golden brown and bubbling. Serve with a large green salad on the side.

Gazpacho salad with pan-fried fish fillets

Gazpacho is an Andalusian cold soup made of raw vegetables. I've reimagined it as a salad here. Mixed bell peppers offer an amazing variety of colours in this recipe, primarily due to their diverse array of carotenoid pigments. Carotenoids help to counteract oxidative stress in our bodies and brains. Many of these carotenoids also act in an anti-inflammatory capacity, which contributes to a lower risk of cardiovascular disease and dementia.

Serves 4

85g sourdough bread, torn into bite-sized chunks

4 tbsp olive oil

4 large tomatoes, cut into chunks

12 large pitted black olives, chopped

1 yellow pepper, deseeded and cut into chunks

1 red pepper, deseeded and cut into chunks

1 red onion, thinly sliced

½ cucumber, cut into chunks

2 garlic cloves, crushed

2 tbsp sherry vinegar

Salt and freshly ground black pepper

4 white fish fillets (such as cod, hake, haddock or pollock)

4 handfuls of watercress

Preheat the oven to 180°C.

Scatter the bread over a baking tray and toss with 1 tablespoon of the oil. Bake in the oven for 10 minutes, until crisp and golden.

Meanwhile, mix together the tomatoes, olives, pepper, onion, cucumber and garlic with another 2 tablespoons of the oil and the sherry vinegar, then season well.

Heat the remaining tablespoon of oil in a large non-stick frying pan over a medium heat. Once the oil is hot, add the fish fillets and fry for 4 minutes, until golden. Flip the fillets over and continue cooking for another 1–2 minutes, until the fish is cooked through.

Quickly mix the croutons with the rest of the salad. Divide between four plates and serve the fish alongside, topped with a handful of watercress.

Prawn and pepper pot

This one-pan wonder is a light evening meal rich in the antioxidant selenium – and it's light on the washing-up too! Selenium is a trace mineral required in only small amounts for health. It helps our body to produce selenoproteins, which are important antioxidant enzymes that help to prevent cell damage by free radicals. Other selenoproteins help to regulate thyroid function and play a role in the immune system.

Serves 4

1 tbsp olive oil

1 onion, finely chopped

1 red pepper, deseeded and sliced

1 green pepper, deseeded and sliced

2 garlic cloves, crushed

1 x 400g tin of chopped tomatoes

250g wild rice

500ml just-boiled water

200g raw peeled prawns, defrosted if frozen

3 handfuls of baby spinach

Toasted pine nuts, to garnish

Heat the oil in a non-stick pan (one with a lid) over a high heat. Add the onion, peppers and garlic and cook for 3 minutes.

Stir in the chopped tomatoes and rice along with the just-boiled water. Cover the pan and continue to cook over a high heat for 12 minutes. Uncover, then stir – the rice should be almost tender.

Stir in the prawns and add a splash more water if the rice is looking dry. Throw the spinach on top and let it wilt for a minute, until the prawns have just turned pink and the rice is tender. Garnish with a few toasted pine nuts.

Baked cod on a bed of ratatouille

Seaweeds are also called sea vegetables. Kombu is a popular one and is a rich source of several minerals, including calcium, magnesium, potassium, copper and iron. Seaweeds also have a high iodine content, especially the brown algae varieties. You only need to use a sprinkling of flakes instead of salt or a few small strips as a garnish on seafood dishes, such as this one.

Serves 4

Olive oil

1 red onion, sliced

1 garlic clove, crushed

3 tomatoes, diced

1 red pepper, deseeded and diced

1 aubergine, diced

1 courgette, diced

Freshly ground black pepper

4 cod fillets

Plain flour, for dusting

Pinch of paprika

Chopped fresh parsley, to garnish

A few strips of kombu seaweed, to garnish (optional)

Sweet potato wedges or boiled baby potatoes, to serve

Preheat the oven to 180°C. Lightly grease a baking tray.

Heat a splash of oil in a large frying pan over a medium heat. Add the onion and garlic and sauté until just cooked, then add all the other vegetables. Cover the pan and cook slowly for about 20 minutes, stirring occasionally. Season with black pepper.

Meanwhile, dust the cod fillets with flour seasoned with paprika. Heat another splash of oil in a non-stick frying pan over a medium heat. Add the fish fillets and pan-fry for 1–2 minutes on each side.

Transfer the fish to the oiled baking tray and finish in the oven for 6–8 minutes, until cooked through.

Divide the ratatouille between four wide, shallow bowls and top with a fish fillet. Garnish with a little chopped fresh parsley and a few strips of kombu seaweed (if using). Serve with chunky sweet potato wedges or boiled baby potatoes.

Spicy Indian fish bake

The glycaemic index is a measure of how fast a carbohydrate-rich food converts to glucose in your body. It's useful to know if you eat foods as a standalone snack, such as an orange or a banana – these have a nice low GI. But potatoes are rarely eaten by themselves. They are part of a meal in this recipe, and it is the glycaemic load that we consider. Enjoy potatoes in moderation and where possible in their jackets as part of a meal to contribute nicely to your potassium, folate, vitamin C and fibre intake. The sweet potato is a great option if you like it, as they're high in beta-carotene, a potent antioxidant.

Serves 4

1 tbsp olive oil

400g sweet potatoes or waxy white potatoes, cut into thick slices or small cubes

1 x 400g tin of chopped tomatoes

100ml vegetable stock

2 garlic cloves, crushed

1 tbsp grated fresh ginger

2 tsp garam masala

1 tsp ground turmeric

1 tsp ground coriander

1 tsp cumin seeds

½ tsp hot chilli powder or chilli flakes

Salt and freshly ground black pepper

1 x 400g tin of chickpeas, drained and rinsed

4 thick white fish fillets (such as cod, hake, haddock or pollock)

A handful of fresh coriander leaves

Steamed greens or a side salad, to serve

Crusty sourdough bread, to serve

Preheat the oven to 180°C.

Pour the tablespoon of oil on your hands, then rub the potatoes to coat them all in the oil. Put into a baking dish, then pour over the tin of chopped tomatoes and vegetable stock. Sprinkle over the garlic, ginger and all the spices and season well, then stir to combine.

Roast in the oven for about 30 minutes. Remove from the oven and stir through the chickpeas.

Season the fish fillets, then place on top of the potato and chickpea mixture and return to the oven to roast for a further 12 minutes.

Sprinkle with fresh coriander leaves and serve with steamed greens or a side salad and some crusty sourdough bread.

Sea bass en papillote with marjoram and lemon

Sometimes white fish needs a lift, and marjoram and lemon do just that. Marjoram is pleasantly aromatic and has some antioxidant activity, arising from several antioxidants, one of which is carnosic acid.

Serves 4

Olive oil, for brushing

4 good-sized sea bass fillets, skinned, or 8 smaller, thinner ones

Salt and freshly ground black pepper

2 carrots, finely shredded (I use a box grater)

2 celery sticks, thinly sliced

4 spring onions, trimmed and thinly sliced

2 tbsp chopped fresh marjoram

8 thin slices of lemon

A little dry white wine or freshly squeezed lemon juice

Preheat the oven to 180°C.

Cut four large rectangles of aluminium foil and four large rectangles of baking parchment big enough to wrap each fish fillet generously. Place each piece of foil on a work surface, shiny side up. Put a piece of parchment on top and fold in the edges, then brush each piece of parchment with a little oil.

Season the sea bass fillets with salt and pepper. Mix all the vegetables together in a bowl and season those too.

Divide the vegetables between the parchment sheets, keeping them to one side of each rectangle of paper to make a bed for the fish fillets. Lay one fillet on top of each bed of vegetables and sprinkle with the marjoram. Put two lemon slices over each fillet and sprinkle with the wine or lemon juice.

Loosely fold the free half of the parchment over the fish and twist or fold the edges tightly together to seal. Put the packets on a baking tray and bake in the oven for 15 minutes (reduce the cooking time if the fillets are smaller).

Serve immediately on warm plates, allowing everyone to open their own fish parcel at the table to avoid it going cold.

White fish parcels with lemony mushroom and herb rice

Supermarkets are now mixing wild rice with both the red and white varieties of quinoa. These carb combos offer more interesting textures and flavours. You can make up your own at home too.

Serves 4

360g wild rice and/or quinoa (or enough for 4 servings)

4 white fish fillets (such as cod, hake, haddock or pollock)

2 lemons, 1 zested and juiced; 1 sliced

Salt and freshly ground black pepper

2 tbsp olive oil

250g mixed mushrooms, sliced

2 garlic cloves, finely chopped

5 tbsp chopped fresh parsley, plus extra to garnish

3 tbsp chopped fresh chives

Green salad, to serve

Preheat the oven to 180°C.

Cook your wild rice and quinoa as per the packet instructions. Drain and set aside.

Place each fish fillet on a square of parchment paper that's three times the size of the fillet. Drizzle the lemon juice over the fillets and season to taste with salt and pepper (or use any combination of sea vegetable flakes, thinly sliced fresh red chilli or fresh ginger). Top each fillet with a slice of lemon and fold into a parcel. Pin with a cocktail stick or secure the parcel so that it doesn't open while cooking. Place the parcels on a baking tray and bake in the oven for 10–15 minutes, depending on the size of the fillets.

Meanwhile, heat the olive oil in a large frying pan over a medium heat. Add the mixed mushrooms and sauté until softened, then stir in the garlic and cook for another minute. Toss the cooked rice, parsley, chives and lemon zest into the mushrooms. Taste and season with a little salt and pepper.

Serve the rice in ramekin dishes beside your white fish parcels and garnish with extra chopped fresh parsley. Serve with a green salad.

Baked sea bass with fennel

The liquorice flavour of fennel helps to give some depth to white fish. This Mediterranean plant is now popular all over the world and continues to be used widely in natural remedies too. The fibre content of fennel helps to prevent a sluggish bowel and supports good gut bacteria. Fibre also helps with weight management and satiety, as it works as a bulking agent in the digestive tract. Fennel and other vegetables and wholegrains can help to reduce appetite, making us feel fuller for longer and thereby reducing our need to snack all day.

Serves 2

4 sea bass fillets, skin on

Salt and freshly ground black pepper

1 fennel bulb, thinly sliced

1 lemon, sliced

A large handful of pitted black olives

A handful of fresh basil leaves, roughly torn

1 tbsp olive oil

Preheat the oven to 180°C.

Rinse the fish fillets, then pat dry with kitchen paper. Season all over, then top two of the fillets with some fennel slices, lemon slices and basil. Scatter the olives and any leftover fennel, lemon and basil in a roasting tin.

Place another two fillets of sea bass on top to sandwich together and place in the roasting tin. Drizzle with the oil and bake in the oven for 20–30 minutes, until cooked through and starting to brown.

Fresh mackerel with sticky honey, sesame and rice wine vinegar dressing

Oily fish, such as mackerel, is a great source of vitamin B12, an essential vitamin for a healthy brain and nervous system. Many typical Western diets are low in omega-3 fatty acids, a key structural component of brain cell membranes and nerve cells. Including one to two oily fish dishes a week is a great way to get these vital nutrients as well as vitamin D.

Serves 4

1–2 tbsp olive oil

4 fillets of fresh mackerel, skin on

Sea salt

1 tbsp toasted sesame seeds, to garnish

For the dressing:

2 tbsp toasted sesame oil

2 tbsp honey

1 tbsp rice wine vinegar

½ clove garlic, finely chopped

To make the dressing, put all the ingredients in a small pot. Bring to the boil and allow to reduce until the sauce thickens (it should coat the back of a spoon). This can be made while the mackerel is cooking.

To cook the mackerel, heat a heavy-based non-stick pan over a high heat, then add the olive oil. Allow the oil to get very hot. Season the mackerel with sea salt, then place in the pan, skin side down, and reduce the heat to medium. Cook for 4 minutes without moving the fish – this will help to achieve a nice crust on the outside and a moist texture on the inside. Turn the mackerel over and cook the other side for 2 minutes.

Pat off the excess oil and place the mackerel on a platter. Spoon over the warm dressing and garnish with toasted sesame seeds.

Salmon with coriander dressing

There are so many wonderful nutrients in oily fish, especially vitamin D and omega-3 fatty acids, which are in short supply in many diets. It's interesting that major fish-eating countries like Japan and Iceland have lower rates of seasonal affective disorder (SAD) in spite of their northern latitudes with long periods of darkness. SAD is a form of depression that normally begins in autumn and continues throughout the winter months. It can affect up to 10% of people and is associated with vitamin D deficiency. Symptoms include feeling sad or anxious, tiredness, poor concentration, irritability and feelings of hopelessness. The exact cause of SAD is unclear, although many studies have suggested that the condition may be triggered by lack of sunlight.

Serves 4

2 tbsp olive oil

2 tsp ground cumin

1 tsp smoked paprika

Salt and freshly ground black pepper

1 x 800g skin-on salmon fillet (large enough to serve 4)

1 lemon, cut into wedges, for serving

For the dressing:

2 large handfuls of fresh coriander, leaves and stems chopped

6 spring onions, finely chopped

1 garlic clove, crushed

2 tbsp olive oil

1 tbsp white wine vinegar

Preheat the oven to 180°C.

Combine the oil, cumin and paprika in a small bowl and season with salt and pepper.

Season the salmon with salt and pepper and place in a baking dish or on a rimmed baking sheet, then drizzle with the spiced olive oil. Roast in the oven for 15–20 minutes, until the fish is opaque and just cooked through.

Meanwhile, to make the dressing, combine all the ingredients in a medium bowl. Season with salt and pepper and set aside.

Remove the salmon from the oven and spoon the coriander dressing over the top. Serve with lemon wedges on the side.

Salmon with sweet potato mash

This dish is a good source of anti-inflammatory essential omega-3 fatty acids and is low in saturated fat.

Serves 4

Vegetables of your choice, e.g. red, orange and yellow peppers, red onions, courgettes, parsnips, carrots, celery, chopped olives or capers

1 tbsp olive oil

1 tbsp runny honey

2 garlic cloves, crushed

A few sprigs of fresh rosemary

4 salmon steaks

Squeeze of lemon or lime juice

Chilli flakes, to taste

Freshly ground black pepper

2 sweet potatoes

1 tbsp natural yogurt

Fresh thyme leaves, to garnish

Preheat the oven to 180°C.

Choose your winter vegetables from the fridge, chop them up and throw them into a roasting tin in a single layer.

Mix the oil with the honey and drizzle it over the vegetables. Add the garlic and a few sprigs of rosemary to the tin.

Roast in the oven for about 30 minutes. Give the veg a quick shake on the tray halfway through the cooking time and add a little more olive oil if necessary.

Meanwhile, wrap four salmon steaks in individual foil parcels with a squeeze of lemon or lime juice, some chilli flakes and lots of freshly ground black pepper. Put in the oven 10 minutes after your roasted vegetables and cook for 20 minutes.

While the vegetables are roasting, peel and steam the sweet potatoes until tender. Mash with a little natural yogurt to give it extra creaminess.

Serve the roasted vegetables with a dollop of the rich, creamy sweet potato mash and a salmon steak alongside. Garnish with another pinch of chilli flakes and a few fresh thyme leaves.

Salmon and farro salad

Oily fish such as salmon is a good source of docosahexaenoic acid (DHA), one of two main omega-3 fatty acids. DHA is a major structural component of the brain – it accounts for the majority of all omega-3 fatty acids in the brain. Insufficient DHA is a risk factor in depression, premature brain ageing and cognitive decline, dementia and Alzheimer's disease.

Serves 4

3 tbsp olive oil

1 onion, finely chopped

Salt and freshly ground black pepper

300g farro, rinsed and drained

500ml water

Zest and juice of 1 lemon

3 mini seedless cucumbers

1 small head of radicchio (140g)

A large handful of fresh dill, chopped

2 tbsp extra virgin olive oil, plus extra for drizzling

4 x 110g boneless salmon fillets, each 2.5cm thick

Heat the 3 tablespoons of regular olive oil in a pan with a lid over a medium heat. Add the onion and some salt and pepper and cook, stirring often, for about 3 minutes. Add the farro and cook, stirring, for about 2 minutes, until the pan is dry and the farro smells toasty. Stir in the water and bring to the boil, then cover, reduce the heat to medium-low and simmer for 20 minutes. Uncover the farro – most of the water should have been absorbed and the grains should be al dente.

Meanwhile, place the lemon zest and juice into a large bowl. Cut the cucumbers in quarters lengthwise, then slice crosswise and add to the bowl. Quarter and core the radicchio, then thinly slice and add to the bowl. Add the dill, extra virgin olive oil and a pinch of salt and pepper and toss until evenly coated.

When the farro is done, season the salmon with salt and pepper, then set it on top of the farro in a single layer, skin side up if applicable. Cover and steam for 8–10 minutes, until the fish is cooked through. Remove from the heat.

Divide the farro and salmon between four wide, shallow bowls and top with the cucumber salad. Drizzle with olive oil and season with salt and pepper to taste.

Herby halibut steak

Citrus flavours are amongst the most preferred internationally. Citrus fruits such as lemons and oranges not only taste great with white fish, but they are good for us too. They provide a rich source of vitamins, minerals and fibre that are essential for normal growth and development and overall nutritional wellbeing. These nutrients and other biologically active non-nutrient compounds found in citrus can also help to reduce the risk of many physical and mental diseases.

Serves 4

1 x 800g fillet of halibut (large enough to serve 4)

Salt and freshly ground black pepper

2 lemons, thinly sliced, plus 1 tbsp lemon juice

1 blood orange or regular orange, thinly sliced

A few fresh thyme sprigs

A few fresh rosemary sprigs

Olive oil, for drizzling

4 handfuls of fresh herbs, such as parsley, coriander, dill and tarragon, leaves picked from the stems

Preheat the oven to 180°C.

Season the halibut with salt and pepper on both sides. Place in a large baking dish with the sliced lemons and orange and the thyme and rosemary sprigs. Drizzle the fish with olive oil.

Bake in the oven for 25–35 minutes, until it is just starting to turn opaque around the edges and is nearly cooked through.

Toss the handfuls of fresh herbs with the tablespoon of lemon juice and a pinch of salt, then scatter on top of the halibut.

Niçoise toasts

When you don't feel like cooking, this timeless Mediterranean salad is super as an open-faced sandwich. Use garlic-infused olive oil on the sourdough toast and plenty of parsley and capers. Capers are the immature green flower buds of a thorny plant that grows both wild and in cultivation throughout the Mediterranean. They are handpicked, sun-dried and then pickled, typically in salted vinegar or brine. A teaspoon has very few calories and tiny amounts of nutrients. They do contain some potentially beneficial compounds, but we are not likely to eat enough in one sitting to get appreciable amounts. We can say the same thing about herbs and spices if we eat them only occasionally. However, a meal pattern containing regular and frequent amounts of all of these protective plant compounds adds up to a lower risk of disease.

Serves 4

4 slices of wholemeal sourdough bread

Garlic-infused olive oil, for drizzling

3 tbsp olive oil, plus a little extra to drizzle

12 anchovy fillets from a jar, drained

1 small red onion, finely chopped

2 garlic cloves, crushed

1 x 400g tin of chopped tomatoes

Handful of fresh parsley, chopped

2 tbsp tomato purée

4 tsp capers, drained

Pinch of chilli flakes

16 pitted Kalamata olives, chopped

2 tbsp finely grated Parmesan cheese

Tiny fresh basil leaves, to serve

Preheat the oven to 180°C.

Place the bread slices on a large baking tray in a single layer and drizzle with garlic-infused olive oil. Toast in the oven for 5 minutes, until slightly dry, taking care not to let the bread burn or become too hard.

Heat the regular olive oil in a non-stick pan over a low heat. Add the anchovies, onion and garlic and cook for 3–4 minutes, until softened, stirring until the anchovies break up. Add the tomatoes, parsley, tomato purée, capers and chilli flakes and cook for 10 minutes, stirring regularly, until the sauce is thick.

Spread a little tomato sauce on each piece of bread and top with some chopped olives. Sprinkle with the Parmesan, then heat under the grill for a minute or two. Garnish with basil and a drizzle of extra virgin olive oil.

Seared tuna with hot pepper sauce

Tuna is a wonderful, nutritious seafood, providing protein, vitamin D, omega-3 fats and selenium. The nutty flavour and pleasantly chewy texture of wild rice goes well with it. Wild rice is a bit more expensive than plain rice, but a little goes a long way. You can also blend wild rice with other types of rice if you like. Nutritionally speaking, wild rice contains more protein and fibre than white rice. It also contains a small amount of several B vitamins, including niacin and B6.

Serves 4

4 fresh tuna steaks

1 tbsp olive oil, plus extra for drizzling

1 red onion, finely chopped

1 red pepper, deseeded and finely chopped

1 celery stick, finely chopped

2 fresh red chillies, deseeded and finely chopped

1 x 400g tin of chopped tomatoes

Juice of 1 lemon

2 tsp Worcestershire sauce

4 handfuls of rocket

Chopped fresh parsley, to garnish

Lemon wedges, to serve

Wild rice, to serve

Lightly drizzle the tuna with olive oil and set aside.

To make the sauce, heat 1 tablespoon of oil in a large non-stick pan over a medium heat. Add the onion, red pepper, celery and chillies and cook for 5 minutes to soften them a bit. Add the tomatoes, then increase the heat to high and cook for 8–10 minutes, stirring occasionally. Remove from the heat and stir in the lemon juice and Worcestershire sauce.

Meanwhile, heat a cast iron griddle pan until it's very hot, then place the fish on it. Cook for 2–3 minutes on each side. Remove and keep warm.

Divide the rocket between four warm plates. Place a tuna steak on each plate and spoon the sauce on top. Sprinkle with chopped fresh parsley and serve with lemon wedges and wild rice.

MEAT

Lamb kebabs

A sustainable diet can be achieved without eliminating any food group completely. Lamb is my favourite red meat and we are particularly lucky in this country to have good-quality lamb available to enhance plant-based meals and salads. Lamb has a special depth of flavour and is delicious with fresh herbs. In the traditional Mediterranean fashion, small portions of lamb were served with legumes to make the meat go further. It was a monthly, not a weekly, treat.

Serves 4

2 tbsp coriander seeds

1 tbsp cumin seeds

3 garlic cloves, crushed

Juice of 1 small lemon

2 tbsp olive oil

1 tsp ground cinnamon

Salt and freshly ground black pepper

400g lean lamb (leg or chump)

Fresh coriander leaves, to garnish

Lime wedges, to serve

Pomegranate seeds, to serve

Green salad, to serve

Hummus (page 76), to serve

Toast the coriander and cumin seeds in a dry pan over a medium heat until they start to give off their scent and just start to take on some colour. Remove them from the pan and leave to cool.

Put the crushed garlic in a large bowl. Grind the toasted coriander and cumin seeds in a pestle and mortar, then add to the garlic. Mix in the lemon juice, oil, cinnamon and some salt and pepper.

Cut the lamb into small bite-sized cubes, then add to the spice mixture and toss to coat. Leave to marinate in the fridge overnight if possible, but for at least 1 hour.

Preheat the grill.

Thread the cubes of lamb onto skewers and grill, turning regularly, for about 10 minutes, until the lamb is just cooked through.

Garnish with a few fresh coriander leaves. Serve with lime wedges, pomegranate seeds, a green salad and hummus.

DINNER

Lamb tagine with apricots, almonds and mint

You don't need to travel any further than your local supermarket to discover the delicious flavours and fresh foods associated with the traditional Mediterranean diet. It's not that difficult to bring the remarkable health benefits to your kitchen cupboards, fridge and table every day. Growing your own fresh garden herbs like mint, thyme and rosemary in patio planters can save you considerable amounts of money annually. Mint is thought to increase bile secretion and encourage bile flow, which helps to speed and ease digestion.

Serves 4

2 tbsp olive oil

400g lean lamb (leg or chump), cubed

1 onion, chopped

2 garlic cloves, crushed

500ml lamb or chicken stock

Zest and juice of 1 orange

1 cinnamon stick

1 tsp honey

Salt and freshly ground black pepper

175g ready-to-eat dried apricots

3 tbsp chopped fresh mint

25g ground almonds

25g toasted flaked almonds

Fresh coriander leaves, to garnish

Pomegranate seeds, to garnish

Couscous (50g uncooked weight per person), to serve

Steamed tenderstem broccoli, to serve

Heat the oil in a large casserole. Add the lamb and cook over a medium-high heat for 3–4 minutes, until evenly browned, stirring often. Remove the lamb to a plate using a slotted spoon.

Reduce the heat to medium, then add the onion and garlic to the casserole and cook gently for 5 minutes, until softened. Return the lamb to the casserole.

Add the stock, orange zest and juice, cinnamon stick, honey and some salt and pepper. Bring to the boil, then reduce the heat, cover and cook gently for 1 hour.

Add the apricots and two-thirds of the mint and cook for 30 minutes, until the lamb is tender. Stir in the ground almonds to thicken the sauce.

Scatter the remaining mint and the toasted flaked almonds over the top along with a few fresh coriander leaves and some pomegranate seeds. Serve with couscous and broccoli on the side.

Roast spiced sweet potato and lamb salad with a lemon and mixed seed dressing

Salad dressings don't have to be tricky to make. Quick home-made dressings are fresher and additive free. Classic Mediterranean ingredients include lemon juice, honey, white wine vinegar and olive oil and are good with strong-flavoured leaf salads, such as rocket or kale or this sweet potato and lamb salad.

Serves 4

400g sweet potatoes, peeled and cut into wedges

4 tbsp olive oil

1 tbsp coriander seeds, coarsely crushed

2 heaped tsp harissa powder

400g lamb loin, trimmed of all fat

1 red onion, thinly sliced

1 large carrot, grated

1 yellow pepper, deseeded and cut into thin strips

1 celery stick, peeled and thinly sliced

250g cherry tomatoes

1 bag of mixed salad leaves

A handful of sultanas

For the dressing:

4 tbsp mixed seeds

2 tbsp clear honey

1 tbsp white wine vinegar

1 tbsp lemon juice

Salt and freshly ground black pepper

50ml extra virgin olive oil

Preheat the oven to 180°C.

Place the sweet potato wedges in a bowl with 2 tablespoons of the olive oil, the coriander seeds and harissa. Toss well so that the potatoes are covered with the oil. Place on a baking tray and roast in the oven for about 25 minutes, until tender.

Add the remaining 2 tablespoons of oil to a pan set over a medium heat. When the pan is hot, add the lamb to the pan and brown on all sides. Transfer to a baking sheet, then finish in the oven until it's cooked to your liking − about 8 minutes for medium and approximately 15 minutes for well done. When cooked, remove from the oven and allow to rest for a few minutes.

Meanwhile, to make the dressing, toast the seeds in a hot dry pan, then roughly crush them in a pestle and mortar. Whisk the honey, vinegar, lemon juice and some salt and pepper together, then slowly whisk in the olive oil. Stir in the seeds.

When the sweet potatoes are cooked, place all the other ingredients in a large bowl and dress with a little of the dressing. Place some salad in each bowl and top with the sweet potato. Slice the lamb and place over the dressed salad.

Smoky pork meatballs and butter beans

Stretch out your occasional meat dish with additional plant protein by adding some fibre-rich prebiotic pulses to your dinner plate. Butter beans take up the smoky flavour of these meatballs beautifully.

Serves 3

300g lean pork mince

Salt and freshly ground black pepper

2 tsp olive oil

2 green peppers, deseeded and thinly sliced

1 large red onion, thinly sliced

3 garlic cloves, crushed

1 tbsp smoked paprika

2 x 400g tins of chopped tomatoes

1 x 400g tin of butter beans, drained and rinsed

A large handful of fresh parsley, chopped

Green salad, to serve

Sourdough bread, to serve

Season the pork mince with a little salt and pepper, then shape into small meatballs.

Heat the oil in a large pan over a medium heat. Add the meatballs and cook for 5 minutes, until golden brown all over.

Push the meatballs to one side of the pan, then add the peppers and onion. Cook for a further 5 minutes, stirring now and then, until the veg have softened, then stir in the garlic and paprika. Stir everything around in the pan for 1 minute, then add the tomatoes. Cover with a lid and simmer for 10 minutes.

Stir in the beans and some seasoning, then simmer for a further 10 minutes, uncovered. Just before serving, top with the chopped parsley.

Serve with a dressed green salad and some crusty sourdough for mopping up the smoky sauce.

POULTRY

Chargrilled chicken escalopes with Italian bean, tomato, feta and basil salad

Cannellini beans and other legumes provide a valuable and cost-effective source of protein, iron, some essential fatty acids, soluble and insoluble fibre and micronutrients. They are valuable inclusions in family meals. This recipe uses cannellini beans, which are white beans with the same shape as a kidney bean. They have a mild, nutty taste and creamy texture and are popular in Italian dishes. They hold their shape well and are one of the best white beans for salads and ragouts.

Serves 4

4 boneless, skinless chicken breast fillets

A little olive oil, for brushing

1–2 tbsp sweet or smoked paprika

For the salad:

1 x 400g tin of cannellini beans, drained and rinsed

250g cherry tomatoes on the vine, quartered

200g rocket

120g feta cheese, crumbled

1 red onion, halved and thinly sliced

1 garlic clove, finely chopped

12 pitted black olives, sliced

1 tbsp chopped or torn fresh basil leaves

2 tbsp extra virgin olive oil

1 tbsp lemon juice

1 tsp white wine vinegar

Salt and freshly ground black pepper

Make the salad by mixing all the ingredients together in a bowl. Set aside.

Cut each chicken fillet in half lengthways and place each piece between two sheets of cling film. Lightly bash the chicken with a rolling pin to make thin chicken escalopes. Brush each side with a little olive oil, then sprinkle each side with paprika and rub it in.

Set a chargrill pan over a medium heat until it's hot. Add the chicken and cook for 2–3 minutes on each side, until cooked through.

Serve with the bean, tomato, feta and basil salad.

Lemon and chilli chicken escalopes with mixed bean, wild rice and beetroot salad

Chicken breast escalopes are very quick to cook. They also work well on the barbecue This recipe is big on filling fibre and heart-friendly vitamin E.

Serves 4

2 boneless, skinless chicken breast fillets

1 garlic clove, finely chopped

Juice of ½ lemon

2 tbsp olive oil

Small pinch of chilli flakes

For the salad:

160g cooked beetroot, finely chopped

100g cooked green beans, cut in halves or thirds

50g cooked wild rice

6 dessertspoons tinned chickpeas

6 dessertspoons tinned kidney beans

6 dessertspoons tinned butter beans

2 tbsp chopped fresh parsley

2 tbsp fresh orange juice

2 tbsp olive oil

Salt and freshly ground black pepper

Cut each chicken fillet in half lengthways and place each piece between two sheets of cling film. Lightly bash the chicken with a rolling pin to make thin chicken escalopes.

In a large bowl, mix together the garlic, lemon juice, oil and chilli flakes. Add the chicken to the bowl and coat with the marinade. Place in the fridge for 30 minutes to marinate.

Meanwhile, make the salad by mixing all the ingredients together in a bowl. Set aside.

Cook the chicken on a chargrill pan set over a medium heat or on the barbecue for 2–3 minutes on each side, until cooked through. The key here is not to have the grill so hot that it blackens the meat.

Serve with the mixed bean, wild rice and beetroot salad.

Oriental chicken and vegetable stir-fry

Although not typically Mediterranean, this cooking method sits well with those of us who are time poor and striving to get our seven-a-day. One of the big benefits of stir-frying is that it's a great way to work a medley of nutritious al dente vegetables into the day. Stir-frying keeps the veggies' bright colour and crisp texture, enhancing their appeal. Broccoli, green beans, peppers and mangetout all work well in a stir-fry. The only trick is adding the vegetables that need more cooking time first. Those that need to be only briefly heated go in towards the end.

Serves 4

2 garlic cloves, finely chopped

1 fresh red chilli, deseeded and finely chopped

1 thumb-sized piece of fresh ginger, peeled and finely chopped

Zest and juice of 1 lime

1 tbsp olive oil, plus extra for cooking

Pinch of cayenne pepper

4 boneless, skinless chicken breast fillets

Fresh coriander or parsley, to garnish

For the vegetable stir-fry:

1 fresh red chilli, deseeded and finely chopped

1 thumb-sized piece of fresh ginger, peeled and finely chopped

1 green pepper, deseeded and thinly sliced

A large handful of mangetout

A large handful of green beans

A large handful of broccoli florets

Put the garlic, chilli and ginger in a large bowl with the lime juice, olive oil and cayenne pepper. Mix well until thoroughly combined.

Using a sharp knife, make two or three incisions in each chicken fillet to allow the marinade to penetrate. Put the chicken in the marinade and leave for at least 20 minutes or overnight.

Preheat the oven to 180°C.

Heat a pan with a little oil. Add the chicken breasts and brown on both sides for 2–3 minutes, then transfer to a baking tray. Bake in the oven for about 12 minutes, until cooked through.

Meanwhile, put the chilli and ginger for the stir-fry in the pan you cooked the chicken in and cook for 2 minutes on a medium-high heat. Next add the green pepper, mangetout, green beans and broccoli and cook for a further 5 minutes. If necessary, add 1 tablespoon of water during the cooking process to stop the vegetables from burning.

Serve the vegetables on a large serving platter with the chicken on top. Garnish with some sprigs of fresh coriander or parsley.

Tasty marinades

Marinades can transform a boring chicken breast into a herb-intense experience. For a small enough effort, marinades provide big payoffs at the dinner table. They give you a great opportunity to be creative too – once you have the marinade basics down, you can experiment with the ingredients. Marinades add flavour and zest to meats. They also add moisture and help to tenderise meats. Furthermore, they reduce the production of potentially cancer-causing compounds in barbecued meats. Even briefly marinating meats can reduce harmful heterocyclic amines (HCAs), which are potentially cancer causing, by as much as 95%. The marinade may act as a barrier or the protective properties may be found in ingredients such as vinegar, citrus juice, herbs, spices and olive oil. And marinating isn't limited to meat – vegetables can be marinated too.

Mediterranean lemon marinade

Zest and juice of 1 lemon

2 garlic cloves, crushed

Freshly ground black pepper

1 sprig of fresh rosemary, chopped

Mix together all the ingredients. Marinate your chicken for up to 12 hours or fish for just 1 hour. Cook on the grill or barbecue.

Minty yogurt marinade

Zest and juice of 1 lemon

2 tbsp natural yogurt

Freshly ground black pepper

4 tbsp chopped fresh mint

Mix the lime zest and juice, yogurt, seasoning and half the mint. Spoon the marinade over chicken and leave for 30 minutes. Cook on a moderate to hot grill, turning occasionally. Sprinkle with the remaining mint and serve with new potatoes and veg or salad.

Desserts

Baked nectarines with almonds and Marsala

I always include fruit, nuts and seeds in desserts where possible. Seasonal fibre-rich fruit (nectarines, apricots, peaches, cherries, figs and grapes) makes a wonderful foundation for many of the old traditional Mediterranean recipes. Fruit's natural sweetness means you can cut back on the added sugar. Nuts (especially almonds) and seeds also add tremendously to the fibre content of your dish. Make your own adaptations and cut the added sugar even further if you want to. However, if you keep your portion small, fully savour and enjoy the occasional treat. There's no room for guilt at the table.

Serves 6

6 nectarines, halved and stones removed

75g amaretti biscuits

75g butter, softened

65g ground almonds

50g golden caster sugar

1 egg

1–2 tbsp toasted flaked almonds

250ml Marsala wine

Greek yogurt, to serve

Preheat the oven to 180°C.

Sit the nectarine halves snugly in a baking dish, cut side up.

Put the amaretti biscuits in a large bowl and use the end of a rolling pin to bash into crumbs. Add the softened butter, ground almonds, caster sugar and egg and stir together.

Push spoonfuls of the mixture into the cavities of the nectarines, piling more on top until the mixture is evenly divided between them. Scatter with the flaked almonds, then carefully pour the Marsala into the dish through a gap between the fruit so that the topping doesn't get soggy.

Bake in the oven for up to 40 minutes, until the topping is golden and crisp and the fruit is soft. Eat warm with the juices spooned over and a dollop of Greek yogurt alongside.

Baked peaches with blueberries and raspberries

A serving of this dessert has a whopping 8g of fibre, a feast for your microbiome. Our target is 25g per day, but many commercially available desserts have little or no fibre. Happy gut microbes produce vitamin K, many B vitamins and short chain fatty acids (SCFAs). They also help to maintain a healthy gut–brain axis with a well-regulated immune system.

Serves 4

55g whole blanched almonds, chopped

5 ripe but firm peaches

6 amaretti biscuits, crumbled

5 dried apricots, diced

Zest and juice of 1 orange

1 egg white

2 tbsp Cointreau

1 tbsp local honey

1 small tray of blueberries

1 small tray of raspberries

Greek or natural yogurt, to serve

Preheat the oven to 180°C.

Place the almonds on a tray and toast in the oven for about 3 minutes, until lightly browned. Set aside to cool.

Cut the peaches in half and remove the stones. Finely dice one peach and set the rest aside.

Mix the diced peach with the chopped almonds, amaretti biscuits, apricots, orange zest, egg white and Cointreau. Fill the peach hollows with the almond mixture and place the halves in a baking dish, stuffed side up. Sprinkle over the orange juice and a drizzle of local honey.

Cover the dish with foil and bake in the oven for 25–30 minutes, until the peaches begin to soften. Remove the foil and increase the oven temperature to 200°C. Throw in the blueberries and raspberries and bake for a further 5 minutes, until the topping is lightly browned. Serve with a tablespoon of Greek or natural yogurt.

Grilled mango

Sometimes the old fruit bowl is difficult to approach on dark winter nights. When you want something deliciously sweet and caramelised in minutes and without any fuss, try grilling your fruit! And don't forget the yogurt. In 2017, researchers claimed to have reversed depression symptoms in mice by feeding them *Lactobacillus*, a probiotic bacteria found in live cultured yogurt. The University of Virginia School of Medicine discovered a specific mechanism for how the bacteria affect mood, pointing to a direct link between the health of the gut microbiome and mental health, which is very promising for human health.

Serves 2

1 ripe mango

2 tsp brown sugar

Greek or natural yogurt, to serve

Cut the mango in half lengthways, avoiding the pit in the middle. Score criss-cross lines across the flesh with a knife. Sprinkle with brown sugar and place flesh side up under a hot grill, until the sugar begins to caramelise.

Remove from the grill and serve with a blob of Greek or natural yogurt.

Easy baked pears

Simple but delicious. Ricotta is an Italian cheese made from the whey protein left over from the production of other sheep, cow or goat cheeses. The whey becomes acidic through a fermentation process where it is left to sit for up to 24 hours at room temperature. It goes beautifully with the almonds in amaretti biscuits and the antioxidant-rich pear. A meal pattern rich in antioxidants helps to mop up free radicals, protecting brain cells against disease.

Serves 4

4 ripe pears

120g ricotta cheese

1–2 tsp ground cinnamon

Honey, for drizzling

8 amaretti biscuits

Preheat the oven to 190°C.

Cut each pear in half, then place them cut side up on a large baking sheet. Use a teaspoon to scoop out the cores and make a dip in the centre of each. Dollop about one teaspoon of ricotta into each dip, then sprinkle over the cinnamon and drizzle with a little honey.

Roast the pears in the oven for 10 minutes.

Meanwhile, put the biscuits in a ziplock bag and use a rolling pin to crush them lightly. Remove the pears from the oven, then scatter the crumbs over each pear.

Return to the oven for another 10 minutes, until the pears are soft and the biscuits are golden brown. Serve drizzled with a little more honey.

Apricot fool

Fresh apricots are divine but hard to come by all year round. If they are in season, stone them, simmer them gently in 2 tablespoons of apple juice and use as described here.

This small fruit has big benefits. Dried versions still contain the fibre and many protective phytonutrients, such as flavonoids. A meal pattern rich in flavonoids can improve numerous cognitive skills, including memory, learning and decision-making, and can also help to prevent age-related mental decline.

Serves 4

175g dried apricots

200ml apple juice or water

Finely grated zest of 1 lemon

500ml Greek or natural yogurt

4 dessertspoons chopped mixed nuts

Oat biscuits, to serve

Put the apricots in a saucepan with the apple juice or water and simmer gently for 10–12 minutes, until the apricots are soft but not overcooked. Roughly mash or blend the apricots to a purée. Set aside to cool.

Add the lemon zest to the yogurt and mix together. Roughly fold the apricots into the yogurt mix. Add 3 dessertspoons of the chopped mixed nuts halfway through folding in, then spoon into four dessert glasses and chill for 2 hours.

Top each glass with the remaining nuts and serve two small oat biscuits alongside.

Fruit and fibre flapjacks

The fastest way to use up opened seeds, nuts and dried fruit before
the best-before date arrives is to make a large tray of nutty treats.
These keep well in an airtight tin in case you get a snack attack. Yes,
there is added sugar in the condensed milk, but the trick is to cut the
flapjacks into small squares. Apart from the condensed milk, all other
ingredients have a myriad of gut-friendly soluble and insoluble fibre
and antioxidant-rich vitamins and minerals. What I really like about this
one is that it takes seconds to make and you might even coax a younger
member of the family to help.

Makes up to 16 squares

1 x 400g tin of
condensed milk

250g oats

150g dried cranberries
or other dried fruit of
choice

150g unsalted roughly
chopped nuts (walnuts,
hazelnuts, pecans)

125g mixed seeds
(pumpkin, sunflower,
sesame)

Preheat the oven to 130°C. Oil a 23cm x 33cm x 4cm
baking tray.

Warm the condensed milk in a large pan.

Meanwhile, mix together all the other ingredients, then
add the warmed condensed milk and stir to combine.

Spread the mixture into the tray and press down with a
spoon or spatula to even the surface.

Bake in the oven for 1 hour. Remove from the oven and
allow to sit for about 15 minutes, then cut into four
across and four down to make 16 chunky bars. Allow the
bars to cool completely before removing from the tin so
that they stay hard and don't break as easily.

Fruit parcels

This healthy and delicious recipe is easy peasy! A selection of ripe fruit of your choice, such as peaches, pears, apricots and plums, works well, but you can use any mix you like in this recipe. A regular intake of vegetables and fruits such as berries helps to protect the brain from chronic inflammation. It also helps to protect against Alzheimer's and Parkinson's diseases by clearing the brain of toxic proteins. The flavonoids in berries can play an important role in removing toxic metals from brain cells.

Serves 4

1 pear

1 apple

1 plum

1 peach

30g mixed berries

4 star anise

4 tsp local honey, plus extra to serve

½ tsp ground cinnamon per parcel

4 tbsp brandy or liqueur

4 tbsp Greek or natural yogurt, to serve

Preheat the oven to 180°C.

Cut all the fruit into wedges and remove any stones or seeds.

Divide all the fruit, star anise, honey and cinnamon into four portions. Place each portion of fruit onto a large piece of parchment paper or foil. Wrap up in parcels, making sure to seal all the edges well, leaving just one small gap or opening at the side. Pour 1 tablespoon of the brandy into each parcel through the gap.

Bake in the oven for about 15 minutes, until the fruit is soft. Serve with some local honey and yogurt.

Index